Contents

U.S. DEPARTMENT OF JUSTICE
OFFICE OF COMMUNITY ORIENTED POLICING SERVICES
Office of the Director
145 N Street, N.E., Washington, DC 20530

Dear colleagues,

In 2004, the COPS Office sponsored a National Summit on Campus Public Safety to explore strategies for colleges and universities in a homeland security environment. The summit afforded an unprecedented opportunity for delegates from the campus public safety field to assess and document existing community policing strategies at colleges and universities. One of the recommendations resulting from this collaborative was that "every agency and organization committed to the safety and well-being of the nation's college and university campuses should adopt a goal to overcome fragmentation by elevating professionalism within police and security operations, increasing internal and external awareness, creating a sense of community, and implementing quality programs that foster consistency and collaboration."

In response to this recommendation, and the events on our nation's colleges and universities involving persons who engage in threatening and volatile behaviors, the COPS Office took action.

In 2008, we funded Margolis Healy & Associates to assist colleges and universities with the adoption and implementation of campus threat assessment programs, policies, and evaluations by hosting seminars throughout the country. This training program, developed by noted campus safety and threat assessment experts, was the first ever national curriculum that focused on a multidisciplinary approach to threat assessment. Furthermore, the curriculum models the ideals of community oriented policing, as it recommends bringing together various constituent groups to act in a proactive manner to prevent potential violence on campuses and provides aid to campus community members who may be in need of assistance.

This guide is a powerful training tool to assist campus threat assessment teams with self-guided opportunities to develop, refine, and enhance their behavioral threat assessment processes. Its design will help teams ensure they have a working knowledge of the nature and process of violence, how to identify persons at risk, reporting and assessing concerns, and resolving situations through compassionate and effective approaches.

Sincerely,

Bernard M. Melekian, Director
Office of Community Oriented Policing Services

Acknowledgments

Without the significant contributions of every member of the original curriculum development team—before, during, and after the development of
the initial curriculum and early direction for this guide—we could not have
developed this tool that should be instrumental in enhancing campus safety.

The COPS Office and principles of Margolis Healy & Associates would like to
thank all of the curriculum development team members and support personnel for their dedication, time, and effort:

Cynthia Pappas
U.S. Department of Justice
Office of Community Oriented Policing Services
Senior Social Science Analyst/Program Manager

Gary J. Margolis, Ed.D.
Managing Partner, Co-Director, CTA Grant
Margolis Healy & Associates

Steven J. Healy
Managing Partner, Co-Director, CTA Grant
Margolis Healy & Associates

Jeff Allison
Special Adviser on Campus Public Safety and Senior Policy Analyst
Office of Law Enforcement Coordination
Federal Bureau of Investigation
Subject Matter Expert

Eugene Deisinger, Ph.D.
Deputy Chief of Police and Director of Threat Management Services
Virginia Polytechnic Institute and State University
Subject Matter Expert

Jeffrey J. Nolan, Esq.
Partner
Dinse, Knapp and McAndrew, P.C.
Subject Matter Expert

Jennifer A. Panagopoulos, Ph.D.
President
Xero Associates, Inc.
Curriculum Development Specialist

Jeffrey W. Pollard, Ph.D., ABPP
Executive Director
Counseling and Psychological Services
George Mason University
Subject Matter Expert

Marisa Randazzo, Ph.D.
Managing Partner
SIGMA Threat Management Associates
Subject Matter Expert

Pamela J. Rypkema, J.D.
Risk Manager
Gallaudet University
Subject Matter Expert

Annie Stevens, Ed.D.
Assistant Vice President for Student Affairs
The University of Vermont
Subject Matter Expert

Katherine Forman
Project Manager
Margolis Healy & Associates

We also would like to thank those who were directly involved in the development of this guide:

Gary J. Margolis, Ed.D.
Managing Partner, Co-Director, CTA Grant
Margolis Healy & Associates

Steven J. Healy
Managing Partner, Co-Director, CTA Grant
Margolis Healy & Associates

Jeffrey J. Nolan, Esq.
Partner
Dinse, Knapp and McAndrew, P.C.
Subject Matter Expert

Marisa Randazzo, Ph.D.
Managing Partner
SIGMA Threat Management Associates
Subject Matter Expert

Annie Stevens, Ed.D.
Assistant Vice President for Student Affairs
The University of Vermont
Subject Matter Expert

Preface

Since the tragic events at Virginia Tech in April 2007, Northern Illinois University in February 2008, and the University of Alabama Huntsville in February 2010, it is uniformly acknowledged that higher education institutions must develop a behavioral threat assessment capacity. Following the incident at Virginia Tech, more than 20 institutional, state, professional association, and governmental reports have recommended that colleges and universities develop and implement threat assessment and management processes and tools as one way to enhance campus safety and security. The report of the Virginia Tech Review Panel[1] called for institutions of higher education to implement systems that link troubled students to appropriate medical and counseling services either on or off campus, and to balance the individual's rights with the rights of all others for safety. Furthermore, the report stated:

> *Incidents of aberrant, dangerous, or threatening behavior must be documented and reported immediately to a college's threat assessment group, and must be acted upon in a prompt and effective manner to protect the safety of the campus community.[2]*

The "Report of the Gubernatorial Task Force for University Campus Safety" recommended:

> *That each college and university develop a multidisciplinary crisis management team, integrating and ensuring communication between the university law enforcement or campus security agency, student affairs, residential housing, counseling center, health center, legal counsel, and any other appropriate campus entities to review individuals and incidents which indicate "at risk" behavior. The team should facilitate the sharing of information, timely and effective intervention, and a coordinated response when required.[3]*

Similarly, the National Association of Attorneys General (NAAG) stated in the "Task Force on School and Campus Safety" report:

> *After hearing from experts and reviewing a number of sources, the Task Force is convinced that schools and colleges cannot rely on unilateral threat assessment by teachers and other school personnel, but rather need to establish a system whereby all disturbing behavior by persons at the school or on the campus is reported to a "vortex" comprised of a central individual or team of individuals with expertise and training in threat assessment.[4]*

Following this trend, in early 2008 the Commonwealth of Virginia enacted a law requiring every public college and university in Virginia to establish a threat assessment team and violence prevention committee.[5] Similarly, the State of Illinois has enacted legislation to develop, in part, "an interdisciplinary and multi-jurisdictional campus violence prevention plan,

---

1.   *Mass Shootings at Virginia Tech, April 16, 2007: Report of the Review Panel* (Virginia Tech Review Panel, 2007), 53, www.governor.virginia.gov/tempcontent/techpanelreport.cfm.

2.   Ibid.

3.   *Report of the Gubernatorial Task Force for University Campus Safety* (2007), 6–7, http://cra20.humansci.msstate.edu/ Florida%20Campus%20Violence%20Report.pdf.

4.   NAAG, *Task Force on School and Campus Safety* (Washington, D.C.: National Association of Attorneys General, 2007), 3, www.ag.arkansas.gov/pdfs/FINAL_REPORT_090407.pdf.

5.   "Violence Prevention Committee; Threat Assessment Team," Legislative Information System, Virginia General Assembly, http://leg1.state.va.us/cgi-bin/legp504.exe?000+cod+23-9.2C10.

including coordination of and communication between all available campus and local mental health and first-response resources…."[6]

As universities and colleges continue to work to develop and implement threat assessment systems in light of evolving best practices, there has been a noted void for quality training based on best and promising practices in threat assessment and management. Furthermore, there are few study guides and other tools that intact assessment teams can use to enhance their threat assessment and management capacity and skills.

Without standardized training on campus threat assessment procedures, examples of successful threat assessment teams and intervention strategies, and workable solutions for common problems, colleges and universities may fail in their efforts to identify and intervene effectively with concerning situations and persons on campus.

Fortunately, the U.S. Department of Justice, Office of Community Oriented Policing Services (COPS Office) recognized and acted on this need by funding the program, "Campus Threat Assessment Training: A Multidisciplinary Approach for Institutions of Higher Education." The COPS Office selected Margolis Healy & Associates to develop and deliver higher-education-focused behavioral threat assessment seminars and this case study guide. The training program and its associated manual, developed by noted campus safety and threat assessment experts, are based on a multidisciplinary approach to threat assessment. They are specifically designed for higher education administrators involved in threat assessment on their campuses, including campus public safety and local law enforcement, faculty, staff, student affairs professionals, counseling center staff, campus judicial officers, campus risk management professionals, and higher education attorneys.

The approach highlighted in the training program and this self-facilitated guide both model the ideals of community oriented policing, as it recommends bringing together various constituent groups to act in a proactive manner to prevent potential violence on campuses and provides assistance to campus community members who may be in need of assistance. A multidisciplinary approach to campus threat assessment epitomizes community policing and, when successfully done, relies upon collaboration and partnerships within the campus community and sometimes with the local community.

To be successful, a highly functioning team must work to eliminate the stovepipes that sometimes plague the routine work on our campuses. Team members using this guide will learn important skills to enhance campus safety and security. Our communities are relying on us to follow this path.

---

6. "Public Act 095-0881," Illinois General Assembly, effective January 1, 2009, www.ilga.gov/legislation/publicacts/fulltext. asp?Name=095-0881.

How to Use This Guide

This guide will allow threat assessment team members to explore and practice threat assessment through small and large group exercises using pre-developed case studies. The overall objective of the guide is to strengthen team members' comprehension and application of the threat assessment principles proscribed in "Campus Threat Assessment Training: A Multidisciplinary Approach for Institutions of Higher Education," a program developed by Margolis Healy & Associates and funded by the COPS Office.

The case studies presented here serve as a guided approach to the four parts of the threat assessment process and illustrate the principles of threat assessment in practical exercises.

After working through several of the case studies, team members should be able to:

- Apply the four-part process designed to (1) identify persons of concern; (2) gather information and investigate; (3) assess information and the situation; and (4) manage the person and situation to reduce the overall threat and get appropriate help
- Apply the mental health violence risk assessment approach and process
- Apply the campus threat assessment and management approach

While it is important to understand the specific steps in the threat assessment and management process, it is critical to understand and adhere to its fundamentals and guiding principles to maximize the opportunity for a positive outcome. The foundation creates the basis upon which to conduct a thorough threat assessment inquiry, make an accurate evaluation, and effectively intervene when necessary to reduce any threat posed.

Disclaimer

While the scenarios included in this guide are comprised of fictitious characters, the facts related to them come from actual cases that various contributors have experienced or managed during their careers.

Facilitator Instructions

For the case studies in this guide, the facilitator should lead each case by reading the initial report to the team and then, through progressive disclosure, provide the Source Information that the team requests. For example, if the team asks to talk with the professors of the person in question, the facilitator should (1) use the table of contents listed at the beginning of each case study to find the page that contains the requested information and (2) read that specific information to the team. The facilitator should read only the information the team requests at that time.

Once the team believes it has sufficient information, or depletes sources to consult, the team should proceed to the Key Investigative Questions[7] and Classification Decision sections. Copies of these two sections should be given to the team at the start of the case study.

Next Step:

Before proceeding to the case studies, read the following aloud to the team:

General Guidelines for Conducting Inquiries

Team members should keep in mind the following as they proceed through the case study:

1. Recognize that violence is a dynamic process. It stems from an interaction between a person, his or her situation, the potential target, and his or her setting.
2. Avoid relying on single factors.
3. Utilize multiple collateral data sources that are credible and possess first-hand knowledge, and then evaluate and minimize the impact of bias.
4. Assess the impact of the investigative process on the person in question and his or her situation.
5. Focus on the facts specific to the case.
6. Focus on the person's behavior rather than the person's traits.
7. Focus on understanding the context of the behavior.
8. Examine the progression of the behavior over time.
9. Corroborate critical information.
10. Every team member's opinion matters and should be shared.
11. Focus on prevention not prediction.
12. The goal is the safety of the community and of the person in question.

---

7.   The Key Investigative Questions were originally developed in Fein, Robert A., Bryan Vosskuil, William S. Pollack, Randy Borum, William Modzeleski, and Marisa Reddy, *Threat Assessment in Schools: A Guide to Managing Threatening Situations and to Creating Safe School Climates* (Washington, D.C.: U.S. Secret Service and U.S. Department of Education, 2002).

Case Study 1 – Michael Chu

Initial Report

Facilitator: Print copies of the Key Investigative Questions and Classification Decision sections and distribute them to the team. Then read aloud the following report and questions to the team.

Michael Chu is a 21-year-old junior. His psychology of religion professor, Dr. Joseph Albritton, contacted the dean of students (although not on the assessment team, the dean of students has direct access to the team) because recent e-mails from Chu expressed increasing hostility toward the professor. Albritton asked Chu to stop by his office yesterday afternoon, so they could discuss the e-mails and Chu's declining grades. Albritton said the conversation was largely one-sided, with Chu just listening. Albritton said that late last night he received a hostile e-mail in which Chu told the professor he "better watch out" if he gave Chu a bad grade. Albritton decided to report this to the dean of students because it troubled him. The dean of students in turn reported this information to the threat assessment team.

Initial Team Questions

1. Based on the information provided, what is the first step the team should take?
2. Is there an imminent situation or a need for the team to call for immediate law enforcement intervention?
3. Is there a need for the team to gather information?
4. If so, where should the team look for information? (Report source requests to the case study facilitator.)

Next Step:

Proceed to the following section: Source Information.

Source Information

Facilitator: Read each source below only when requested by the team; if the team does not think to check certain sources or interview certain people, do not read that information aloud.

Dean of Students

The dean of students said she knows Michael Chu fairly well. She led a two-week student trip over the summer to Israel, and Chu was on the trip. Although he was new to the university (he had just transferred and was about to start his first semester at the time of the trip), she feels he has made an effort to make friends and generally is a nice person. She expressed surprise that Chu would act in any sort of threatening manner. She also mentioned that Professor Albritton has a reputation for being a very tough grader and some students have accused him of being unfair.

Other Professors

Economics 201 (Micro-Economics) Professor – Chu's economics professor said that Chu has fallen asleep a few times in class in the past two or three weeks but that several students fall asleep in class regularly and he doesn't think it is all that concerning.

Social Psychology Professor – Chu's social psychology professor said that Chu has been doing about average in the class and has seen no concerning behavior. The professor also said the course is a large class and that there are many students he doesn't know well, including Chu.

Geography 101 Professor – Chu's geography professor said that recently Chu has seemed distracted throughout many classes and has been curt in some responses but not hostile. She added that on a few recent occasions she has had to call Chu's name several times before he seemed to hear her and respond to her question.

Roommate

Chu's roommate has been very worried about Chu's behavior over the last few weeks but wasn't sure what to do about it. He thought about telling someone but didn't know if he should talk to someone in Residence Life, to the dean of students, or with some of his friends. Chu has been staying up most nights and not sleeping. He says things that sound outrageous, like his claim that he's being told to do certain things by the CIA and that he will be punished if he doesn't follow the CIA's instructions. The roommate said that Chu often leaves their room in the middle of the night, but he doesn't know where Chu goes. He also said that Chu seems pretty angry with one of his professors and has said the guy "better watch it."

Campus Public Safety

The campus public safety department has no record of Chu. He has no criminal record within the state, and there is no record of registered weapons.

Parents/Family

Chu has lived with his older, adult cousin during vacations and summers. His cousin said that he is not allowed at his parents' house because the parents fear for their safety when he stops taking his medication. His cousin said she is able to get along well with Chu when he takes his medication but that lately she has been worried that he is starting to unravel again the way he did at his last school. She said he had to be hospitalized at this last school and was involuntarily committed there for three months before being released.

Next Step:

Proceed to the following sections: Key Investigative Questions and then Classification Decision. Make sure the team possesses copies of the pages within these sections.

Key Investigative Questions

As a team, discuss the following specific questions[8] to organize and evaluate the information gathered on the person/situation of concern:

1. **What are Michael Chu's motives and goals?**

   ▪ What motivated him to make the statements or take actions that caused him to come to the attention of the team?

   ▪ Does the situation or circumstance that led to these statements or actions still exist?

   ▪ Does he have a major grievance or grudge? Against whom?

   ▪ What efforts have been made to resolve the problem, and what has been the result? Does he feel that any part of the problem is resolved or see any alternatives?

2. **Have there been any communications suggesting ideas or an intent to attack?**

   ▪ What, if anything, has Chu communicated to someone else (e.g., targets, friends, co-workers, faculty, and family) or written in a diary, journal, e-mail, or website concerning his grievances, ideas, and/or intentions?

   ▪ Have friends been alerted or warned away?

3. **Has Chu shown inappropriate interest in any of the following?**

   ▪ Workplace, school, or campus attacks or attackers

   ▪ Weapons (including recent acquisition of any relevant weapon)

   ▪ Incidents of mass violence (e.g., terrorism, workplace violence, and mass murderers)

4. **Has Chu engaged in attack-related behaviors?** This means any behavior that moves an idea of violence toward actual violence. Such behaviors might include:

   ▪ Developing an attack idea or plan

   ▪ Making efforts to acquire or practice with weapons

   ▪ Surveying possible sites and areas for attack

   ▪ Testing access to potential targets

   ▪ Rehearsing attacks or ambushes

5. **Does Chu have the capacity to carry out an act of targeted violence?**

   ▪ How organized is his thinking and behavior?

   ▪ Does he have the means (e.g., access to a weapon) to carry out an attack?

6. **Is Chu experiencing hopelessness, desperation, and/or despair?**

   ▪ Is there information to suggest that he is experiencing desperation and/or despair?

   ▪ Has he experienced a recent failure, loss, and/or loss of status?

   ▪ Is he known to be having difficulty coping with a stressful event?

   ▪ Has he engaged in behavior that suggests he has considered ending his life?

---

8. Source: Fein et al., *Threat Assessment in Schools* (see n. 7).

7. **Does Chu have a trusting relationship with at least one responsible or trustworthy person?**
   - Does he have at least one person he can confide in and believe that person will listen without judging or jumping to conclusions?
   - Is he emotionally connected to other people?
   - Has he previously come to someone's attention or raised concern in a way that suggests he needs intervention or supportive services?

8. **Does Chu see violence as the acceptable, desirable, or only way to solve problems?**
   - Does the setting around him (e.g., friends, co-workers, students, parents, and teachers) explicitly or implicitly support or endorse violence as a way of resolving problems or disputes?
   - Has he been "dared" by others to engage in an act of violence?

9. **Are Chu's conversation and story consistent with his actions?**
   - If there is an interview with Chu, is his story consistent with behaviors observed by others?

10. **Are other people concerned about Chu's potential for violence?**
    - Are those who know him concerned that he might take action based on violent ideas or plans?
    - Are those who know him concerned about a specific target?

11. **What circumstances might affect the likelihood of violence?**
    - What factors in Chu's life and/or environment might increase or decrease the likelihood that he will engage in violent behavior?
    - What is the response of others who know about Chu's ideas or plans? (Do they actively discourage him from acting violently, encourage him to attack, deny the possibility of violence, or passively collude with an attack?)

12. **Where does Chu exist along the "pathway toward violence"?**
    - Has he:
      - Developed an idea to engage in violence?
      - Developed a plan?
      - Taken any steps toward implementing a plan?
      - Developed the capacity or means to carry out the plan?
    - How fast is he moving toward engaging in violence?
    - Where can the team intervene to move Chu off the pathway toward violence?

Next Step:

Proceed to the following section: Classification Decision.

Classification Decision

Assessment of Person/Situation

Use the gathered information and the answers to the Key Investigative Questions to answer these ultimate questions:

1. **Does Chu pose a threat of harm, whether to himself, to others, or to both? That is, does his behavior suggest that he is on a pathway toward violence?**

   — Has he developed an idea to engage in violence?

   — Has he developed a plan?

   — Has he taken any steps toward implementing the plan?

   — Has he developed the capacity or means to carry out the plan?

   — How fast is he moving toward engaging in violence?

   — Where can the team intervene to move Chu off the pathway toward violence?

2. **If Chu does not pose a threat of harm, does he otherwise show a need for help or intervention, such as mental health care?**

Priority Risk Scale

Decide how urgent or imminent the situation is, and assign the corresponding classification level using the following priority risk scale:[9]

Priority 1 – Extreme Risk

Appears to pose an imminent threat, and needs immediate containment and eventually case management. Procedures include:

- Contact police/campus security immediately to contain/control person.
- Develop and implement individual case management plan.
- Monitor person, situation, and effectiveness of plan.
- Address any necessary organizational issues.
- Make changes to plan as necessary.
- Discontinue case management when person no longer poses a threat.
- Document investigation, evaluation, plan, and plan implementation.

Priority 2 – High Risk

Appears to pose a non-imminent threat, and requires case management intervention. Procedures include:

- Develop and implement individual case management plan.
- Monitor person, situation, and effectiveness of plan.
- Address any necessary organizational issues.
- Make changes to plan as necessary.
- Discontinue case management when person no longer poses a threat.
- Document investigation, evaluation, plan, and plan implementation.

---

9.   The priority risk scale was originally developed in Deisinger, Gene, Marisa Randazzo, Daniel O'Neill, and Jenna Savage, *The Handbook for Campus Threat Assessment & Management Teams* (Stoneham, MA: Applied Risk Management, LLC, 2008).

Priority 3 – Moderate Risk

Does not appear to pose a threat at this time, but exhibits behaviors that are likely to be disruptive to the community. Warrants a referral and/or monitoring plan. Procedures include:

- Develop and implement a referral plan to get person connected with resources needed to solve problems.
- Address any necessary organizational issues.
- Monitor person and situation if necessary.
- Document investigation, evaluation, and any referral or monitoring.

Priority 4 – Low Risk

Does not appear to pose a threat at this time, and does not exhibit behaviors that are likely to be disruptive to the community. Warrants a monitoring plan to deter escalation. Procedures include:

- Develop and implement a plan to monitor the person/situation for any change.

Priority 5 – No Identified Risk

Does not appear to pose a threat at this time, and no intervention or monitoring is necessary. Close case after proper documentation.

Case Classification and Rationale

Priority Level _____

_____

_____

_____

_____

_____

_____

_____

_____

_____

_____

_____

_____

_____

Next Step:

Proceed to the following section: Case Management and Monitoring.

Case Management and Monitoring

Facilitator: If the team decides on a classification level that requires a case management plan—or if they choose a lower level but decide to implement some case management measures—the team should develop and plan how to implement and monitor a case management plan. To prompt them to do so, read aloud the following to the team:

Develop an individualized plan for intervention and monitoring based on the investigation information and other facts known about the person in question. When doing so, take into account the following:

- Case management is more art than science.
- The plan must be fact-based and individualized.
- Engagement is essential, even when dealing with someone who appears very angry. Distancing—including through suspension or expulsion—can make monitoring or intervention particularly difficult.
- Personalities matter. Choose someone the person already trusts, or someone he will like.
- Use the "crew resource management" concept:
  - The team leader may make the ultimate decision, but everyone is obligated to share opinions and raise concerns and ideas.
  - Focus on what still works—for the person and his situation.
  - Focus on what the team, or institution, can change or fix.
  - Think creatively about resources, as well as "eyes and ears."
- Anticipate what might change in the short- and mid-term and how the person may react.
- Management options can include any mix of the following:
  - Outpatient counseling or mental health care
  - Emergency psychiatric evaluation
  - Mentoring relationship
  - Academic accommodations (if the student has a documented disability; also consider "academic relief" according to the institution's policy)
  - Suspension or expulsion
  - Voluntary medical leave
  - Changes in systemic problems or situations
  - Social skills training
  - Behavioral contract
  - Family involvement
  - Law enforcement involvement
  - Diversion programs
  - Management by walking around or through appropriate alliances
  - Others
- Monitor using available resources. Who sees the person regularly (on and off campus), on weekends, online, etc.?
- Document decision making, implementation, and progress.

Case Management Plan

_____

_____

_____

_____

_____

_____

_____

_____

_____

_____

_____

_____

_____

_____

_____

Case Study 2 – Dr. Roberta Roberts

Initial Report

Facilitator: Print copies of the Key Investigative Questions and Classification Decision sections and distribute them to the team. Then read aloud the following report and questions to the team.

Dr. Roberta Roberts is an associate professor of philosophy. She is under review for tenure this year and has received the recommendation of her department chair, Professor Cynthia Tally, to be granted tenure. Roberts is aware that her department has recommended her for tenure. However, Tally just notified the threat assessment team that she has been receiving complaints about Roberts' behavior, which has been raising concern among her colleagues in the Philosophy Department. Specifically, some of the other professors and staff in the department have said that Roberts yells and throws things against the wall when she is angry, and some of the staff has called her a "bully." Tally is unsure how long the behavior has gone on because she just took over as department chair this year and that the previous department chair, Professor Bud McAllister, may be able to provide more information. Tally has just learned that the faculty council voted to deny tenure to Roberts and that Roberts will learn of this decision tomorrow morning. Tally has asked the team whether she should be concerned about Roberts.

Initial Team Questions

1. Based on the information provided, what is the first step the team should take?

2. Is there an imminent situation or a need for the team to call for immediate law enforcement intervention?

3. Is there a need for the team to gather information?

4. If so, where should the team look for information? (Report source requests to the case study facilitator.)

Next Step:

Proceed to the following section: Source Information.

Source Information

Facilitator: Read each source below only when requested by the team; if the team does not think to check certain sources or interview certain people, do not read that information aloud.

Professor Bud McAllister, Former Philosophy Department Chair

Professor McAllister said that Dr. Roberts has shown problematic behavior for several years. When Roberts was named an associate professor, her appointment letter contained language indicating that she needed to act "more collegially" around the department. McAllister said that Roberts does great work and has brought in some large grants, which have benefitted the university. His opinion is that the caliber of her work offsets any behavioral concerns and that she is "all bark and no bite."

Other Professors in the Philosophy Department

Two of Roberts' colleagues, both of whom received tenure last year, said that Roberts is gruff and never engages in the social niceties that colleagues in a department try to do. But they feel she isn't a real problem and admire her work. They added that she is in a long-distance relationship with a woman who is a tenured professor at a university across the country and that the relationship seems to be good for her.

Staff Members in the Philosophy Department

Several secretaries in the department expressed concern about Roberts' increasingly belligerent behavior. They said she is bossy and mean and bullies people whom she sees as clearly subordinate to herself. The secretaries said that her behavior seems to have gotten much worse as she gets closer to the tenure decision. They said she is sure she is getting tenure and worry that her behavior will only get worse if she does.

Significant Other

Roberts' significant other, Linda, informed the team that she recently broke off her relationship with Roberts because she could no longer tolerate Roberts' bullying and demeaning behavior. Linda said that the two of them had had a long-distance relationship for five years and that she had always tolerated Roberts' demeaning comments, but in the past few weeks they had become excessive and very mean-spirited. Linda said she felt as if Roberts had become emotionally abusive to her and that she was also fixated on getting tenure. Linda said that Roberts often talked about how she doesn't get the level of respect within the department that she feels she is owed and that tenure would ensure that other professors, staff, and students would pay her that respect. Linda understands that the tenure process can be very stressful, as she went through it herself a few years earlier, but thinks there is something a bit odd or troublesome about how fixated Roberts has become. She added that Roberts had recently completed a job search at other, more research-focused institutions because she isn't sure her current university is the right fit for her. But the job search had yielded only a few interviews and no job offers. As such, Roberts said she is now "stuck" at her current university. Linda also said that Roberts initially took the breakup well, but Linda has begun receiving phone hang-up calls and some weird e-mails from someone she doesn't know and thinks Roberts may be behind both of those incidents.

Campus Public Safety

The campus Public Safety Department has no record of Roberts. She has no criminal record in the state, and there is no record of registered weapons.

Human Resources

Human Resources has had no recent complaints about or issues involving Roberts. The only record they have is of an incident three years ago when Roberts threatened one of the secretaries because she failed to type up her grant application properly. Their records indicate that the dispute was mediated between the two parties and that Roberts was required to take an anger management class. The secretary quit the university the following year and did not leave any contact information.

Online Search

An online search yielded several posts on www.RateMyProfessors.com about Roberts, all of which are negative. The anonymous ratings and comments describe Roberts as egotistical and a bully to her students, especially the ones who seem quiet or meek. A Google search on Roberts' name revealed a blog, which appears to be linked to her personal e-mail address, with negative comments about several faculty members and most of the staff members in her department. Although she does not use their full names—only their initials—and does not name the university, all of the initials used match those of faculty and staff currently in her department. The last two blog posts include the following statements: "I better get tenure if they know what's good for them" and "If I don't get tenure, I wonder if I'll feel like that University of Alabama professor did…"

Next Step:

Proceed to the following sections: Key Investigative Questions and then Classification Decision. Make sure the team possesses copies of the pages within these sections.

Key Investigative Questions

As a team, discuss the following specific questions[10] to organize and evaluate the information gathered on the person/situation of concern:

1. **What are Dr. Roberts' motives and goals?**
   - What motivated her to make the statements or take actions that caused her to come to the attention of the team?
   - Does the situation or circumstance that led to these statements or actions still exist?
   - Does she have a major grievance or grudge? Against whom?
   - What efforts have been made to resolve the problem, and what has been the result? Does she feel that any part of the problem is resolved or see any alternatives?

2. **Have there been any communications suggesting ideas or an intent to attack?**
   - What, if anything, has Roberts communicated to someone else (e.g., targets, friends, co-workers, faculty, and family) or written in a diary, journal, e-mail, or website concerning her grievances, ideas, and/or intentions?
   - Have friends been alerted or warned away?

3. **Has Roberts shown inappropriate interest in any of the following?**
   - Workplace, school, or campus attacks or attackers
   - Weapons (including recent acquisition of any relevant weapon)
   - Incidents of mass violence (e.g., terrorism, workplace violence, and mass murderers)

4. **Has Roberts engaged in attack-related behaviors?** This means any behavior that moves an idea of violence toward actual violence. Such behaviors might include:
   - Developing an attack idea or plan
   - Making efforts to acquire or practice with weapons
   - Surveying possible sites and areas for attack
   - Testing access to potential targets
   - Rehearsing attacks or ambushes

5. **Does Roberts have the capacity to carry out an act of targeted violence?**
   - How organized is her thinking and behavior?
   - Does she have the means (e.g., access to a weapon) to carry out an attack?

6. **Is Roberts experiencing hopelessness, desperation, and/or despair?**
   - Is there information to suggest that she is experiencing desperation and/or despair?
   - Has she experienced a recent failure, loss, and/or loss of status?
   - Is she known to be having difficulty coping with a stressful event?
   - Has she engaged in behavior that suggests she has considered ending her life?

---

10.   Source: Fein et al., *Threat Assessment in Schools* (see n. 7).

7. **Does Roberts have a trusting relationship with at least one responsible or trustworthy person?**

   ■ Does she have at least one person she can confide in and believe that person will listen without judging or jumping to conclusions?

   ■ Is she emotionally connected to other people?

   ■ Has she previously come to someone's attention or raised concern in a way that suggests she needs intervention or supportive services?

8. **Does Roberts see violence as the acceptable, desirable, or only way to solve problems?**

   ■ Does the setting around her (e.g., friends, co-workers, students, parents, and teachers) explicitly or implicitly support or endorse violence as a way of resolving problems or disputes?

   ■ Has she been dared by others to engage in an act of violence?

9. **Are Roberts' conversation and story consistent with her actions?**

   ■ If there is an interview with Roberts, is her story consistent with behaviors observed by others?

10. **Are other people concerned about Roberts' potential for violence?**

   ■ Are those who know her concerned that she might take action based on violent ideas or plans?

   ■ Are those who know her concerned about a specific target?

11. **What circumstances might affect the likelihood of violence?**

   ■ What factors in Roberts' life and/or environment might increase or decrease the likelihood that she will engage in violent behavior?

   ■ What is the response of others who know about Roberts' ideas or plans? (Do they actively discourage her from acting violently, encourage her to attack, deny the possibility of violence, or passively collude with an attack?)

12. **Where does Roberts exist along the "pathway toward violence"?**

   ■ Has she:

      — Developed an idea to engage in violence?

      — Developed a plan?

      — Taken any steps toward implementing a plan?

      — Developed the capacity or means to carry out the plan?

   ■ How fast is she moving toward engaging in violence?

   ■ Where can the team intervene to move Roberts off the pathway toward violence?

Next Step:

Proceed to the following section: Classification Decision.

Classification Decision

Assessment of Person/Situation

Use the gathered information and the answers to the Key Investigative Questions to answer these ultimate questions:

1. **Does Roberts pose a threat of harm, whether to herself, to others, or to both? That is, does her behavior suggest that she is on a pathway toward violence?**

   — Has she developed an idea to engage in violence?

   — Has she developed a plan?

   — Has she taken any steps toward implementing the plan?

   — Has she developed the capacity or means to carry out the plan?

   — How fast is she moving toward engaging in violence?

   — Where can the team intervene to move Roberts off the pathway toward violence?

2. **If Roberts does not pose a threat of harm, does she otherwise show a need for help or intervention, such as mental health care?**

Priority Risk Scale

Decide how urgent or imminent the situation is, and assign the corresponding classification level using the following priority risk scale:[11]

Priority 1 – Extreme Risk

Appears to pose an imminent threat, and needs immediate containment and eventually case management. Procedures include:

- Contact police/campus security immediately to contain/control person.
- Develop and implement individual case management plan.
- Monitor person, situation, and effectiveness of plan.
- Address any necessary organizational issues.
- Make changes to plan as necessary.
- Discontinue case management when person no longer poses a threat.
- Document investigation, evaluation, plan, and plan implementation.

Priority 2 – High Risk

Appears to pose a non-imminent threat, and requires case management intervention. Procedures include:

- Develop and implement individual case management plan.
- Monitor person, situation, and effectiveness of plan.
- Address any necessary organizational issues.
- Make changes to plan as necessary.
- Discontinue case management when person no longer poses a threat.
- Document investigation, evaluation, plan, and plan implementation.

---

11.   Source: Deisinger et al., *Handbook for Campus Threat Assessment* (see n. 9).

Priority 3 – Moderate Risk

Does not appear to pose a threat at this time, but exhibits behaviors that are likely to be disruptive to the community. Warrants a referral and/or monitoring plan. Procedures include:

- Develop and implement a referral plan to get person connected with resources needed to solve problems.
- Address any necessary organizational issues.
- Monitor person and situation if necessary.
- Document investigation, evaluation, and any referral or monitoring.

Priority 4 – Low Risk

Does not appear to pose a threat at this time, and does not exhibit behaviors that are likely to be disruptive to the community. Warrants a monitoring plan to deter escalation. Procedures include:

- Develop and implement a plan to monitor the person/situation for any change.

Priority 5 – No Identified Risk

Does not appear to pose a threat at this time, and no intervention or monitoring is necessary. Close case after proper documentation.

Case Classification and Rationale

Priority Level _____

_____

_____

_____

_____

_____

_____

_____

_____

_____

_____

_____

_____

_____

_____

_____

Next Step:

Proceed to the following section: Case Management and Monitoring.

Case Management and Monitoring

Facilitator: If the team decides on a classification level that requires a case management plan—or if they choose a lower level but decide to implement some case management measures—the team should develop and plan how to implement and monitor a case management plan. To prompt them to do so, read aloud the following to the team:

Develop an individualized plan for intervention and monitoring based on the investigation information and other facts known about the person in question. When doing so, take into account the following:

- Case management is more art than science.
- The plan must be fact-based and individualized.
- Engagement is essential, even when dealing with someone who appears very angry. Distancing—including through suspension or expulsion—can make monitoring or intervention particularly difficult.
- Personalities matter. Choose someone the person already trusts, or someone she will like.
- Use the "crew resource management" concept:
    — The team leader may make the ultimate decision, but everyone is obligated to share opinions and raise concerns and ideas.
    — Focus on what still works—for the person and her situation.
    — Focus on what the team, or institution, can change or fix.
    — Think creatively about resources, as well as "eyes and ears."
- Anticipate what might change in the short- and mid-term and how the person may react.
- Management options can include any mix of the following:
    — Outpatient counseling or mental health care
    — Emergency psychiatric evaluation
    — Mentoring relationship
    — Work-related accommodations
    — Leave of absence (with or without pay)
    — Suspension or expulsion
    — Voluntary medical leave
    — Changes in systemic problems or situations
    — Social skills training
    — Behavioral contract
    — Family involvement
    — Law enforcement involvement
    — Diversion programs
    — Management by walking around or through appropriate alliances
    — Others
- Monitor using available resources. Who sees the person regularly (on and off campus), on weekends, online, etc.?
- Document decision making, implementation, and progress.

Case Management Plan

Case Study 3 – Andy Bell

Initial Report

Facilitator: Print copies of the Key Investigative Questions and Classification Decision sections and distribute them to the team. Then read aloud the following report and questions to the team.

Andy Bell is a recently laid-off staff member of the college's alumni association office. Across the college, approximately 15% of all staff members were laid off due to budget constraints. In Bell's small department, however, he was the only employee over the age of 60 and the only one laid off. As such, Bell believes his layoff was a matter of age discrimination and recently sent several blast e-mails to faculty, staff, and college alumni about how he has been mistreated. The director of the college's alumni association office notified the team that the e-mails are starting to scare some of the staff members in the office. The director said that Bell was always a bit "odd," and some of the staff are worried that he seems like a "rampage shooter." The director thought he should notify the team so they could look into the e-mails and concerns.

Initial Team Questions

1. Based on the information provided, what is the first step the team should take?
2. Is there an imminent situation or a need for the team to call for immediate law enforcement intervention?
3. Is there a need for the team to gather information?
4. If so, where should the team look for information? (Report source requests to the case study facilitator.)

Next Step:

Proceed to the following section: Source Information.

Source Information

Facilitator: Read each source below only when requested by the team; if the team does not think to check certain sources or interview certain people, do not read that information aloud.

E-mails from Andy Bell

In the two weeks since Andy Bell was let go from the college, he has sent five e-mails to a large distribution list of all of the college's current faculty, staff, and administrators and to several prominent alumni (those with track records of giving generous contributions to the college). The content of all of these e-mails appears to be consistent: Bell outlined his allegations of age discrimination and his evidence and said that the college should be "held accountable for its discriminatory actions." The tone of all five e-mails appears consistent: Bell sounds angry at being laid off and certain that the college is wrong in its decision. In the most recent e-mail, Bell said he is intent on publicly humiliating the college unless he gets his job back and "justice is served." He included his e-mail address and phone number at the end of each e-mail and encouraged people to contact him with questions or gestures of support.

Other Alumni Office Staff Members

Two of Bell's female co-workers in the alumni association office expressed significant concern that Bell had been a danger to them. When asked why, one co-worker said it was because she believes Bell is a loner and he had talked about the military often. The other co-worker said she had been concerned because she thinks Bell is "creepy." When asked to clarify why Bell is creepy, the woman said that Bell had asked her on a date a few months prior, but she has no interest and wishes he had never done that. Another office staff member, Glenn, thinks that Bell's e-mails are inappropriate but have a point about the discrimination issue and maybe the college has made a mistake in letting Bell go. Glenn had no concerns about Bell's behavior while he was employed in the office and has had none since Bell left. The department secretary, Millicent, said that Bell is harmless and just seemed a bit lonely sometimes since his wife died a few years ago.

Criminal Records/Weapons Check

Bell has no criminal record in NCIC or the state's criminal database. He is not listed as a party in any lawsuits in the past 10 years. He is not the subject of any restraining orders in the state. He has lived in the same state for the past 26 years.

Campus Public Safety

The campus Public Safety Department has no record of Bell.

Human Resources

Human Resources has had no recent complaints about Bell. His personnel file indicates that he had been employed by the college for 15 years and had received positive performance evaluations every year. He had never been disciplined while employed at the college. His job application and resume from when he applied for the position in the alumni office indicate that he was previously employed by an alumni office at a similar-sized college in the same state and that he sought the new position because he and his wife wanted to move closer to their grandchildren.

Online Search

An online search on Bell's name yielded several possible Facebook pages, all of which are private. It also yielded an obituary for Bell's wife who died of cancer five years ago. The obituary mentions that Bell has three adult children, all of whom live in the area. The obituary also mentions that his wife's memorial service was led by the college chaplain who is described in the obituary as a close friend of the Bell family. No other online information was found about Bell.

An online search on the name of the college yielded several discussion forums about the college, including one with a series of negative comments about the college from someone using the screen name "pops2010." The posts include criticisms of the college for mismanagement, poor leadership, and the recent layoffs. Other screen names posted similar critiques and appear legitimate (i.e., not written by the same person who posts under pops2010). The increase in volume in recent postings on the forums indicates that many people are upset about the college layoffs and feel they were not handled well.

Bell's Adult Children

On behalf of the threat assessment team, the alumni office director reached out to each of Bell's three adult children whom he met on various occasions. He asked each of them how they think Bell is doing since the layoff, and each one told the director the same thing: Bell is angry and feels he has been treated poorly by an employer he worked hard to serve for 15 years. Bell's younger son, Michael—a recent graduate of the college—said he wouldn't be surprised if Bell sues the college and has encouraged Bell to contact the EEOC to find out about his rights under the law.

College Chaplain

The college chaplain declined to say much about Bell, although he did confirm that Bell and his wife have been longtime friends of the chaplain and the chaplain's wife. He also confirmed that he performed Bell's wife's memorial service five years ago. The chaplain said that Bell's wife's death hit him hard initially, but he thinks Bell has recovered well in the past few years. Bell had recently mentioned an interest in wanting to start dating again, which the chaplain thinks is a good thing. He added that Bell would probably respond to the loss of his job with similar strength and resilience, but the chaplain feels it is understandable if Bell continues to be angry for quite some time about being let go.

Interview with Bell

Bell appeared reluctant to agree to an interview but became more inclined to talk when the interviewer made it clear that the interviewer wanted to hear Bell's side of the story. Bell took nearly two hours to tell his story in full, initially appearing quite angry and agitated, but eventually telling the rest in a manner that was calmer and quieter. When asked about his feelings toward the college, Bell said that he started to post nasty comments on several forums (and admitted he uses the screen name "pops2010"), but he feels he was starting to embarrass his youngest son who just graduated from the college, so he stopped posting on those forums. He said he is considering filing a complaint with the EEOC instead to see if they want to take up the matter or at least issue him a right-to-sue letter. When asked about his interest in the military, Bell indicated that he has always wanted to serve in the military but that his eyesight is too poor to do so. He added that his brother had been in the Army and was killed at the beginning of the Vietnam War. When asked if he owns any weapons, Bell said no. When asked if he knows how to fire a gun, Bell said that his brother taught him how to shoot when he was a teenager and they used to go to the firing range together. He said he hasn't touched a gun since his brother was killed and has no interest in them. When asked what he might do next for work, Bell said that he has already been offered a part-time position with a local non-profit organization that helps cancer survivors and thinks he may take that while he looks for full-time work.

Next Step:

Proceed to the following sections: Key Investigative Questions and then Classification Decision. Make sure the team possesses copies of the pages within these sections.

Key Investigative Questions

As a team, discuss the following specific questions[12] to organize and evaluate the information gathered on the person/situation of concern:

1. **What are Bell's motives and goals?**
   - What motivated him to make the statements or take actions that caused him to come to the attention of the team?
   - Does the situation or circumstance that led to these statements or actions still exist?
   - Does he have a major grievance or grudge? Against whom?
   - What efforts have been made to resolve the problem and what has been the result? Does he feel that any part of the problem is resolved or see any alternatives?

2. **Have there been any communications suggesting ideas or an intent to attack?**
   - What, if anything, has Bell communicated to someone else (e.g., targets, friends, co-workers, faculty, and family) or written in a diary, journal, e-mail, or website concerning his grievances, ideas, and/or intentions?
   - Have friends been alerted or warned away?

3. **Has Bell shown inappropriate interest in any of the following?**
   - Workplace, school, or campus attacks or attackers
   - Weapons (including recent acquisition of any relevant weapon)
   - Incidents of mass violence (e.g., terrorism, workplace violence, and mass murderers)

4. **Has Bell engaged in attack-related behaviors?** This means any behavior that moves an idea of violence toward actual violence. Such behaviors might include:
   - Developing an attack idea or plan
   - Making efforts to acquire or practice with weapons
   - Surveying possible sites and areas for attack
   - Testing access to potential targets
   - Rehearsing attacks or ambushes

5. **Does Bell have the capacity to carry out an act of targeted violence?**
   - How organized is his thinking and behavior?
   - Does he have the means (e.g., access to a weapon) to carry out an attack?

6. **Is Bell experiencing hopelessness, desperation, and/or despair?**
   - Is there information to suggest that he is experiencing desperation and/or despair?
   - Has he experienced a recent failure, loss, and/or loss of status?
   - Is he known to be having difficulty coping with a stressful event?
   - Has he engaged in behavior that suggests he has considered ending his life?

---

12.   Source: Fein et al., *Threat Assessment in Schools* (see n. 7).

7. **Does Bell have a trusting relationship with at least one responsible or trustworthy person?**

   ▪ Does he have at least one person he can confide in and believe that person will listen without judging or jumping to conclusions?

   ▪ Is he emotionally connected to other people?

   ▪ Has he previously come to someone's attention or raised concern in a way that suggests he needs intervention or supportive services?

8. **Does Bell see violence as the acceptable, desirable, or only way to solve problems?**

   ▪ Does the setting around him (e.g., friends, co-workers, students, parents, and teachers) explicitly or implicitly support or endorse violence as a way of resolving problems or disputes?

   ▪ Has he been dared by others to engage in an act of violence?

9. **Are Bell's conversation and story consistent with his actions?**

   ▪ If there is an interview with Bell, is his story consistent with behaviors observed by others?

10. **Are other people concerned about Bell's potential for violence?**

   ▪ Are those who know him concerned that he might take action based on violent ideas or plans?

   ▪ Are those who know him concerned about a specific target?

11. **What circumstances might affect the likelihood of violence?**

   ▪ What factors in Bell's life and/or environment might increase or decrease the likelihood that he will engage in violent behavior?

   ▪ What is the response of others who know about Bell's ideas or plans? (Do they actively discourage him from acting violently, encourage him to attack, deny the possibility of violence, or passively collude with an attack?)

12. **Where does Bell exist along the "pathway toward violence"?**

   ▪ Has he:

     — Developed an idea to engage in violence?

     — Developed a plan?

     — Taken any steps toward implementing a plan?

     — Developed the capacity or means to carry out the plan?

   ▪ How fast is he moving toward engaging in violence?

   ▪ Where can the team intervene to move Bell off the pathway toward violence?

Next Step:

Proceed to the following section: Classification Decision.

Classification Decision

Assessment of Person/Situation

Use the gathered information and the answers to the Key Investigative Questions to answer these ultimate questions:

1. **Does Bell pose a threat of harm, whether to himself, to others, or to both? That is, does his behavior suggest that he is on a pathway toward violence?**

   — Has he developed an idea to engage in violence?

   — Has he developed a plan?

   — Has he taken any steps toward implementing the plan?

   — Has he developed the capacity or means to carry out the plan?

   — How fast is he moving toward engaging in violence?

   — Where can the team intervene to move Bell off the pathway toward violence?

2. **If Bell does not pose a threat of harm, does he otherwise show a need for help or intervention, such as mental health care?**

Priority Risk Scale

Decide how urgent or imminent the situation is, and assign the corresponding classification level using the following priority risk scale:[13]

Priority 1 – Extreme Risk

Appears to pose an imminent threat, and needs immediate containment and eventually case management. Procedures include:

- Contact police/campus security immediately to contain/control person.
- Develop and implement individual case management plan.
- Monitor person, situation, and effectiveness of plan.
- Address any necessary organizational issues.
- Make changes to plan as necessary.
- Discontinue case management when person no longer poses a threat.
- Document investigation, evaluation, plan, and plan implementation.

Priority 2 – High Risk

Appears to pose a non-imminent threat, and requires case management intervention. Procedures include:

- Develop and implement individual case management plan.
- Monitor person, situation, and effectiveness of plan.
- Address any necessary organizational issues.
- Make changes to plan as necessary.
- Discontinue case management when person no longer poses a threat.
- Document investigation, evaluation, plan, and plan implementation.

---

13.   Source: Deisinger et al., *Handbook for Campus Threat Assessment* (see n. 9).

Priority 3 – Moderate Risk

Does not appear to pose a threat at this time, but exhibits behaviors that are likely to be disruptive to the community. Warrants a referral and/or monitoring plan. Procedures include:

- Develop and implement a referral plan to get person connected with resources needed to solve problems.
- Address any necessary organizational issues.
- Monitor person and situation if necessary.
- Document investigation, evaluation, and any referral or monitoring.

Priority 4 – Low Risk

Does not appear to pose a threat at this time, and does not exhibit behaviors that are likely to be disruptive to the community. Warrants a monitoring plan to deter escalation. Procedures include:

- Develop and implement a plan to monitor the person/situation for any change.

Priority 5 – No Identified Risk

Does not appear to pose a threat at this time, and no intervention or monitoring is necessary. Close case after proper documentation.

Case Classification and Rationale

Priority Level _____

_____

_____

_____

_____

_____

_____

_____

_____

_____

_____

_____

_____

_____

_____

Next Step:

Proceed to the following section: Case Management and Monitoring.

Case Management and Monitoring

Facilitator: If the team decides on a classification level that requires a case management plan—
or if they choose a lower level but decide to implement some case management measures—
the team should develop and plan how to implement and monitor a case management plan.
To prompt them to do so, read aloud the following to the team:

Develop an individualized plan for intervention and monitoring based on
the investigation information and other facts known about the person in
question. When doing so, take into account the following:

- Case management is more art than science.

- The plan must be fact-based and individualized.

- Engagement is essential, even when dealing with someone who
  appears very angry. Distancing—including through suspension
  or expulsion—can make monitoring or intervention particularly
  difficult.

- Personalities matter. Choose someone the person already trusts,
  or someone he will like.

- Use the "crew resource management" concept:
  - The team leader may make the ultimate decision, but
    everyone is obligated to share opinions and raise concerns
    and ideas.
  - Focus on what still works—for the person and his situation.
  - Focus on what the team, or institution, can change or fix.
  - Think creatively about resources, as well as "eyes and ears."

- Anticipate what might change in the short- and mid-term and how
  the person may react.

- Management options can include any mix of the following:
  - Outpatient counseling or mental health care
  - Emergency psychiatric evaluation
  - Mentoring relationship
  - Suspension or expulsion
  - Voluntary medical leave
  - Changes in systemic problems or situations
  - Social skills training
  - Behavioral contract
  - Family involvement
  - Law enforcement involvement
  - Diversion programs
  - Management by walking around or though appropriate
    alliances
  - Others

- Monitor using available resources. Who sees the person regularly
  (on and off campus), on weekends, online, etc.?

- Document decision making, implementation, and progress.

Case Management Plan

_____

_____

_____

_____

_____

_____

_____

_____

_____

_____

_____

_____

_____

_____

Case Study 4 – Sandy Miller

Initial Report

Facilitator: Print copies of the Key Investigative Questions and Classification Decision sections and distribute them to the team. Then read aloud the following report and questions to the team.

Sandy Miller is a senior art major entering her last semester. She transferred from another college and has been a student here for approximately one year. She is taking a course in forensic science (commonly referred to as "CSI for Credit") to fulfill a degree requirement. Her forensic science professor, Guy Williams, reported to his department chair, Dr. Leslie Bauer, that Miller has been dropping by his office nearly every day since the beginning of the semester and often leaves notes when he is not there. The notes suggest she has a crush on Williams, as they are about personal issues and her admiration for him. Williams also told the department chair that Miller has started appearing at places where he often goes on the weekend, near his apartment, which is several miles away from campus. He does not recall ever mentioning where he lives and has an unlisted address. Bauer said she asked Williams whether he thought Miller might have followed him home one day, but Williams said he doubted it. When he saw Miller at those locations (e.g., a coffee shop and bookstore during the previous weekend and the weekend before that, respectively), Williams said she seemed genuinely surprised to see him there and said her boyfriend lived in the area. At the end of the conversation, Bauer added that she felt it was important for the team to know that she and Williams have been dating for over a year and are quite serious, although they keep their relationship a secret because they both work in the same department and she is his department chair. She said that she felt embarrassed disclosing this information but figured there was a chance the team might find out anyway.

Initial Team Questions

1. Based on the information provided, what is the first step the team should take?

2. Is there an imminent situation or a need for the team to call for immediate law enforcement intervention?

3. Is there a need for the team to gather information?

4. If so, where should the team look for information? (Report source requests to the case study facilitator.)

Next Step:

Proceed to the following section: Source Information.

Source Information

Facilitator: Read each source below only when requested by the team; if the team does not think to check certain sources or interview certain people, do not read that information aloud.

Guy Williams

In talking with Guy Williams, he reiterated the same information that Dr. Leslie Bauer, the department chair, shared in her initial report to the team. Williams said he had never met or seen Sandy Miller prior to having her as a student in his class this semester. But he said that since the semester began he runs into her—near his office, near the department's building on campus, and in the coffee shop and bookstore near his home—several times a week. Guy said he feels bad telling the team about Miller because she seems harmless, and her notes to him sound as if she merely has a crush on him, but Bauer encouraged him to let her call the team because it seems as if these "coincidences" of running into Miller are happening with greater frequency. Miller also recently stayed after class to make an appointment with Williams during his office hours this coming week because she said she has a personal problem and wants to get his advice. Williams said several times that he worries he is making a big deal out of nothing and doesn't want to get Miller into any trouble.

Notes from Miller to Williams

Williams said he threw out most of the notes that Miller left for him on his office door or in his department mail box because they seemed benign, simply saying she'd stopped by to see him and would come back another time. But Williams kept the note Miller left for him this week because he said he was giving serious consideration to Bauer's suggestion that they report Miller's behavior to the threat assessment team and figured the team would probably want to see them. The note says:

"Hi Guy (I'm so glad you encouraged me to call you by your first name!), I stopped by again but you weren't here. I am really looking forward to our meeting next week. I know you'll be able to help me out with this problem I'm facing. You are so smart and caring, I just know you'll have great advice! See you SOON! Sandy ♡ ."

Criminal Record

Miller has no known criminal record, and the local police department has had no interactions with her.

Campus Public Safety

The campus Public Safety Department has no record of Miller.

Student Affairs

The dean of students said that Miller is relatively unknown. She appears to be doing quite well in her academic courses, and the dean noted that most of the credits from her previous college were accepted, so she lost little ground in terms of credits needed to graduate when she transferred. Miller has not been subject to any student conduct proceedings since starting as a student at the college. Her file includes a copy of a request for a roommate change that was submitted by her roommate the previous year, with a notation that the change was made at the end of the previous semester and both girls were moved to separate single rooms that had become available.

Online Search

An online search on Miller's name located her Facebook page, which is set to private, and a MySpace page that appears not to have been updated in two years.

An online search on Williams' name yielded several ratings on www.RateMyProfessor.com that include the following comments: "Prof Williams is hot, hot, HOT," "Talk about babe-a-licious…," and "He'll make dem good girls go bad." The postings appear to come from different people (they are posted by different screen names). The first and second postings were made during the previous semester. The third posting was made two weeks ago. The search on Williams' name also located an apparent fan site for him on Facebook, with the page appearing similar to fan pages created for celebrities on Facebook. There are several recent photos of Williams, all of which seem as if he was unaware his picture was being taken. When asked about the Facebook fan page, Williams said he had no idea the page existed and doesn't know who created it.

Miller's Former Roommate

Miller's former roommate, Michelle Costello, was initially difficult to reach because she graduated the previous semester, and the college has only her parents' home number. After finally reaching Costello, she was reluctant to talk about Miller because she said she is worried about what Miller might do if she finds out that Costello spoke to the team about her. After being reassured that the team would not need to tell Miller with whom they spoke, Costello said that she requested a change of roommate the previous semester because she felt that Miller was starting to act weird. Miller seemed quite interested in a young man who worked at the Starbucks in town and started going there several times a week, then every day, and eventually several times a day, always while the young man was working. Costello said that initially she thought it was just a crush, but she became concerned when Miller spoke about the man as if he were in love with her. She became worried when Miller doctored photos she had taken of the young man using Photoshop and created pictures that looked as if Miller and the young man were in the photos together. Costello said that as soon as she saw those photos framed on Miller's nightstand, she called the Residential Life Office to request a roommate change; she admits that she never explained to the Residential Life Office staff why she wanted the switch. She just said that she wanted a single room because she wanted a quieter environment during the pressures of her last semester. Costello said that she was so glad she requested the switch because right before she moved out, Miller discovered the Starbucks guy had a girlfriend and became irate, telling Costello that "no one else can have him [the Starbucks guy]." Costello added that the only thing that made her feel better about Miller was that she had been seeing a counselor at the college counseling center for a while, and Costello assumed the counselor knew about the Starbucks guy and was treating Miller's obsession with him.

Previous College—Initial Outreach

The team chair reached out to the dean of students at Miller's previous college and was told that they can't share any information about Miller because the information is protected by FERPA. A follow-up call from the college legal counsel to the dean of students at Miller's previous college has not been returned.

Previous College—Second Outreach to Different Department

The team chair asked the director of Public Safety to contact the chief of the police department at Miller's previous college. The chief indicated that they are quite familiar with Miller and that she left the college after being told she would face a student conduct proceeding and possible criminal charges if she stayed. The chief explained that Miller had been stalking the wife of a professor because she was romantically interested in him and believed that he was in love with her, too. Miller also felt that the wife was in the way and started pursuing and harassing her. The chief said their investigation suggested that perhaps there had been some romantic involvement between the professor and Miller initially, but that the professor eventually rejected her, and that was when she started pursuing the professor's wife. The chief said that the college essentially reached a deal with Miller in which she agreed to go away if everyone stayed quiet.

Miller's Counselor at College Counseling Center

Miller's counselor said he cannot confirm that she is one of his patients and asked that the team not contact him unless it has a release from Miller allowing disclosure of confidential health and mental health information.

Weapons Check

A search of registered weapons nationwide finds a hit on Miller's name in the state where she previously went to college. From the application form, it appears that Miller purchased the firearm around the same timeframe that the chief at her previous college described her pursuing the professor's wife. She has not registered the weapon in the state where she is currently in college, so whether she still has the weapon is unclear.

Interview with Miller

Miller refuses to speak with anyone from the team and said she is going to call her lawyer because she feels the college is harassing her.

Next Step:

Proceed to the following sections: Key Investigative Questions and then Classification Decision. Make sure the team possesses copies of the pages within these sections.

Key Investigative Questions

As a team, discuss the following specific questions[14] to organize and evaluate the information gathered on the person/situation of concern:

1. **What are Miller's motives and goals?**

   ▓ What motivated her to make the statements or take actions that caused her to come to the attention of the team?

   ▓ Does the situation or circumstance that led to these statements or actions still exist?

   ▓ Does she have a major grievance or grudge? Against whom?

   ▓ What efforts have been made to resolve the problem and what has been the result? Does she feel that any part of the problem is resolved or see any alternatives?

2. **Have there been any communications suggesting ideas or an intent to attack?**

   ▓ What, if anything, has Miller communicated to someone else (e.g., targets, friends, co-workers, faculty, and family) or written in a diary, journal, e-mail, or website concerning her grievances, ideas, and/or intentions?

   ▓ Have friends been alerted or warned away?

3. **Has Miller shown inappropriate interest in any of the following?**

   ▓ Workplace, school, or campus attacks or attackers

   ▓ Weapons (including recent acquisition of any relevant weapon)

   ▓ Incidents of mass violence (e.g., terrorism, workplace violence, and mass murderers)

4. **Has Miller engaged in attack-related behaviors?** This means any behavior that moves an idea of violence toward actual violence. Such behaviors might include:

   ▓ Developing an attack idea or plan

   ▓ Making efforts to acquire or practice with weapons

   ▓ Surveying possible sites and areas for attack

   ▓ Testing access to potential targets

   ▓ Rehearsing attacks or ambushes

5. **Does Miller have the capacity to carry out an act of targeted violence?**

   ▓ How organized is her thinking and behavior?

   ▓ Does she have the means (e.g., access to a weapon) to carry out an attack?

6. **Is Miller experiencing hopelessness, desperation, and/or despair?**

   ▓ Is there information to suggest that she is experiencing desperation and/or despair?

   ▓ Has she experienced a recent failure, loss, and/or loss of status?

   ▓ Is she known to be having difficulty coping with a stressful event?

   ▓ Has she engaged in behavior that suggests she has considered ending her life?

---

14.   Source: Fein et al., *Threat Assessment in Schools* (see n. 7).

7. **Does Miller have a trusting relationship with at least one responsible or trustworthy person?**
   - Does she have at least one person she can confide in and believe that person will listen without judging or jumping to conclusions?
   - Is she emotionally connected to other people?
   - Has she previously come to someone's attention or raised concern in a way that suggests she needs intervention or supportive services?

8. **Does Miller see violence as the acceptable, desirable, or only way to solve problems?**
   - Does the setting around her (e.g., friends, co-workers, students, parents, and teachers) explicitly or implicitly support or endorse violence as a way of resolving problems or disputes?
   - Has she been dared by others to engage in an act of violence?

9. **Are Miller's conversation and story consistent with her actions?**
   - If there is an interview with Miller, is her story consistent with behaviors observed by others?

10. **Are other people concerned about Miller's potential for violence?**
   - Are those who know her concerned that she might take action based on violent ideas or plans?
   - Are those who know her concerned about a specific target?

11. **What circumstances might affect the likelihood of violence?**
   - What factors in Miller's life and/or environment might increase or decrease the likelihood that she will engage in violent behavior?
   - What is the response of others who know about Miller's ideas or plans? (Do they actively discourage her from acting violently, encourage her to attack, deny the possibility of violence, or passively collude with an attack?)

12. **Where does Miller exist along the "pathway toward violence"?**
   - Has she:
     - Developed an idea to engage in violence?
     - Developed a plan?
     - Taken any steps toward implementing a plan?
     - Developed the capacity or means to carry out the plan?
   - How fast is she moving toward engaging in violence?
   - Where can the team intervene to move Miller off the pathway toward violence?

Next Step:

Proceed to the following section: Classification Decision.

Classification Decision

Assessment of Person/Situation

Use the gathered information and the answers to the Key Investigative Questions to answer these ultimate questions:

1. **Does Miller pose a threat of harm, whether to herself, to others, or to both? That is, does her behavior suggest that she is on a pathway toward violence?**

   — Has she developed an idea to engage in violence?

   — Has she developed a plan?

   — Has she taken any steps toward implementing the plan?

   — Has she developed the capacity or means to carry out the plan?

   — How fast is she moving toward engaging in violence?

   — Where can the team intervene to move Miller off the pathway toward violence?

2. **If Miller does not pose a threat of harm, does she otherwise show a need for help or intervention, such as mental health care?**

Priority Risk Scale

Decide how urgent or imminent the situation is, and assign the corresponding classification level using the following priority risk scale:[15]

Priority 1 – Extreme Risk

Appears to pose an imminent threat, and needs immediate containment and eventually case management. Procedures include:

- Contact police/campus security immediately to contain/control person.
- Develop and implement individual case management plan.
- Monitor person, situation, and effectiveness of plan.
- Address any necessary organizational issues.
- Make changes to plan as necessary.
- Discontinue case management when person no longer poses a threat.
- Document investigation, evaluation, plan, and plan implementation.

Priority 2 – High Risk

Appears to pose a non-imminent threat, and requires case management intervention. Procedures include:

- Develop and implement individual case management plan.
- Monitor person, situation, and effectiveness of plan.
- Address any necessary organizational issues.
- Make changes to plan as necessary.
- Discontinue case management when person no longer poses a threat.
- Document investigation, evaluation, plan, and plan implementation.

---

15.   Source: Deisinger et al., *Handbook for Campus Threat Assessment* (see n. 9).

Priority 3 – Moderate Risk

Does not appear to pose a threat at this time, but exhibits behaviors that are likely to be disruptive to the community. Warrants a referral and/or monitoring plan. Procedures include:

- Develop and implement a referral plan to get person connected with resources needed to solve problems.
- Address any necessary organizational issues.
- Monitor person and situation if necessary.
- Document investigation, evaluation, and any referral or monitoring.

Priority 4 – Low Risk

Does not appear to pose a threat at this time, and does not exhibit behaviors that are likely to be disruptive to the community. Warrants a monitoring plan to deter escalation. Procedures include:

- Develop and implement a plan to monitor the person/situation for any change.

Priority 5 – No Identified Risk

Does not appear to pose a threat at this time, and no intervention or monitoring is necessary. Close case after proper documentation.

Case Classification and Rationale

Priority Level _____

_____

_____

_____

_____

_____

_____

_____

_____

_____

_____

_____

_____

_____

_____

Next Step:

Proceed to the following section: Case Management and Monitoring.

Case Management and Monitoring

Facilitator: If the team decides on a classification level that requires a case management plan—or if they choose a lower level but decide to implement some case management measures—the team should develop and plan how to implement and monitor a case management plan. To prompt them to do so, read aloud the following to the team:

Develop an individualized plan for intervention and monitoring based on the investigation information and other facts known about the person in question. When doing so, take into account the following:

- Case management is more art than science.

- The plan must be fact-based and individualized.

- Engagement is essential, even when dealing with someone who appears very angry. Distancing—including through suspension or expulsion—can make monitoring or intervention particularly difficult.

- Personalities matter. Choose someone the person already trusts, or someone she will like.

- Use the "crew resource management" concept:
  — The team leader may make the ultimate decision, but everyone is obligated to share opinions and raise concerns and ideas.
  — Focus on what still works—for the person and her situation.
  — Focus on what the team, or institution, can change or fix.
  — Think creatively about resources, as well as "eyes and ears."

- Anticipate what might change in the short- and mid-term and how the person may react.

- Management options can include any mix of the following:
  — Outpatient counseling or mental health care
  — Emergency psychiatric evaluation
  — Mentoring relationship
  — Academic accommodations (if the student has a documented disability; also consider "academic relief" according to the institution's policy)
  — Suspension or expulsion
  — Voluntary medical leave
  — Changes in systemic problems or situations
  — Social skills training
  — Behavioral contract
  — Family involvement
  — Law enforcement involvement
  — Diversion programs
  — Management by walking around or through appropriate alliances
  — Others

- Monitor using available resources. Who sees the person regularly (on and off campus), on weekends, online, etc.?

- Document decision making, implementation, and progress.

Case Management Plan

_____

_____

_____

_____

_____

_____

_____

_____

_____

_____

_____

_____

_____

_____

_____

Case Study 5 – Todd Smith

Initial Report

Facilitator: Print copies of the Key Investigative Questions and Classification Decision sections and distribute them to the team. Then read aloud the following report and questions to the team.

Laura Smith, a secretary in the president's office, is in the process of leaving her husband, Todd Smith, of 17 years. The campus public safety director informs the team (of which she is a member) that her liaison at the local police department said that Laura recently got a restraining order against her husband. According to the police liaison, Laura testified that Todd had beaten her on several occasions, with the most recent beating (one month ago) resulting in an overnight hospitalization for her. The public safety director is under the impression that Laura plans to move out of her house within the next week.

Initial Team Questions

1. Based on the information provided, what is the first step the team should take?

2. Is there an imminent situation or a need for the team to call for immediate law enforcement intervention?

3. Is there a need for the team to gather information?

4. If so, where should the team look for information? (Report source requests to the case study facilitator.)

Next Step:

Proceed to the following section: Source Information.

Source Information

Facilitator: Read each source below only when requested by the team; if the team does not think to check certain sources or interview certain people, do not read that information aloud.

Laura Smith

Laura Smith confirmed she just got a restraining order against her husband, Todd Smith, but said that she did so only as a precautionary measure. She said that her husband is only bad when he drinks and he can drink only at night because of his job as a security guard for a local company. Laura said that her husband knows she is moving out, and he knows he has to stay away from her from now on. She also said that her husband is embarrassed about his behavior and has said that he'll never get that rough with her again.

Todd Smith's Supervisor

Todd Smith's supervisor said that the company recently fired Todd because of the restraining order—the company policy states that no armed security guards may have restraining orders against them. The supervisor said that Todd seemed surprisingly calm at being fired, almost as if he expected it.

Laura Smith's Supervisor

Laura Smith's supervisor confirmed that Laura has had several one- and two-day absences in the past six to eight weeks, including one right after the weekend that corresponds with the dates of her most recent beating and hospitalization.

Online Search

An online search on Laura Smith's name yielded no information. An online search on Todd Smith's name yielded no information.

Next Step:

Proceed to the following sections: Key Investigative Questions and then Classification Decision. Make sure the team possesses copies of the pages within these sections.

Key Investigative Questions

As a team, discuss the following specific questions[16] to organize and evaluate the information gathered on the person/situation of concern:

1. **What are Todd Smith's motives and goals?**
   - What motivated him to make the statements or take actions that caused him to come to the attention of the team?
   - Does the situation or circumstance that led to these statements or actions still exist?
   - Does he have a major grievance or grudge? Against whom?
   - What efforts have been made to resolve the problem and what has been the result? Does he feel that any part of the problem is resolved or see any alternatives?

2. **Have there been any communications suggesting ideas or an intent to attack?**
   - What, if anything, has Smith communicated to someone else (e.g., targets, friends, co-workers, faculty, and family) or written in a diary, journal, e-mail, or website concerning his grievances, ideas, and/or intentions?
   - Have friends been alerted or warned away?

3. **Has Smith shown inappropriate interest in any of the following?**
   - Workplace, school, or campus attacks or attackers
   - Weapons (including recent acquisition of any relevant weapon)
   - Incidents of mass violence (e.g., terrorism, workplace violence, and mass murderers)

4. **Has Smith engaged in attack-related behaviors?** This means any behavior that moves an idea of violence toward actual violence. Such behaviors might include:
   - Developing an attack idea or plan
   - Making efforts to acquire or practice with weapons
   - Surveying possible sites and areas for attack
   - Testing access to potential targets
   - Rehearsing attacks or ambushes

5. **Does Smith have the capacity to carry out an act of targeted violence?**
   - How organized is his thinking and behavior?
   - Does he have the means (e.g., access to a weapon) to carry out an attack?

6. **Is Smith experiencing hopelessness, desperation, and/or despair?**
   - Is there information to suggest that he is experiencing desperation and/or despair?
   - Has he experienced a recent failure, loss, and/or loss of status?
   - Is he known to be having difficulty coping with a stressful event?
   - Has he engaged in behavior that suggests he has considered ending his life?

---

16.   Source: Fein et al., *Threat Assessment in Schools* (see n. 7).

7. **Does Smith have a trusting relationship with at least one responsible or trustworthy person?**
   - Does he have at least one person he can confide in and believe that person will listen without judging or jumping to conclusions?
   - Is he emotionally connected to other people?
   - Has he previously come to someone's attention or raised concern in a way that suggests he needs intervention or supportive services?

8. **Does Smith see violence as the acceptable, desirable, or only way to solve problems?**
   - Does the setting around him (e.g., friends, co-workers, students, parents, and teachers) explicitly or implicitly support or endorse violence as a way of resolving problems or disputes?
   - Has he been dared by others to engage in an act of violence?

9. **Are Smith's conversation and story consistent with his actions?**
   - If there is an interview with Smith, is his story consistent with behaviors observed by others?

10. **Are other people concerned about Smith's potential for violence?**
    - Are those who know him concerned that he might take action based on violent ideas or plans?
    - Are those who know him concerned about a specific target?

11. **What circumstances might affect the likelihood of violence?**
    - What factors in Smith's life and/or environment might increase or decrease the likelihood that he will engage in violent behavior?
    - What is the response of others who know about Smith's ideas or plans? (Do they actively discourage him from acting violently, encourage him to attack, deny the possibility of violence, or passively collude with an attack?)

12. **Where does Smith exist along the "pathway toward violence"?**
    - Has he:
        — Developed an idea to engage in violence?
        — Developed a plan?
        — Taken any steps toward implementing a plan?
        — Developed the capacity or means to carry out the plan?
    - How fast is he moving toward engaging in violence?
    - Where can the team intervene to move Smith off the pathway toward violence?

Next Step:

Proceed to the following section: Classification Decision.

Classification Decision

Assessment of Person/Situation

Use the gathered information and the answers to the Key Investigative Questions to answer these ultimate questions:

1. **Does Smith pose a threat of harm, whether to himself, to others, or to both? That is, does his behavior suggest that he is on a pathway toward violence?**

   — Has he developed an idea to engage in violence?

   — Has he developed a plan?

   — Has he taken any steps toward implementing the plan?

   — Has he developed the capacity or means to carry out the plan?

   — How fast is he moving toward engaging in violence?

   — Where can the team intervene to move Smith off the pathway toward violence?

2. **If Smith does not pose a threat of harm, does he otherwise show a need for help or intervention, such as mental health care?**

Priority Risk Scale

Decide how urgent or imminent the situation is, and assign the corresponding classification level using the following priority risk scale:[17]

Priority 1 – Extreme Risk

Appears to pose an imminent threat, and needs immediate containment and eventually case management. Procedures include:

- Contact police/campus security immediately to contain/control person.
- Develop and implement individual case management plan.
- Monitor person, situation, and effectiveness of plan.
- Address any necessary organizational issues.
- Make changes to plan as necessary.
- Discontinue case management when person no longer poses a threat.
- Document investigation, evaluation, plan, and plan implementation.

Priority 2 – High Risk

Appears to pose a non-imminent threat, and requires case management intervention. Procedures include:

- Develop and implement individual case management plan.
- Monitor person, situation, and effectiveness of plan.
- Address any necessary organizational issues.
- Make changes to plan as necessary.
- Discontinue case management when person no longer poses a threat.
- Document investigation, evaluation, plan, and plan implementation.

---

17.   Source: Deisinger et al., *Handbook for Campus Threat Assessment* (see n. 9).

Priority 3 – Moderate Risk

Does not appear to pose a threat at this time, but exhibits behaviors that are likely to be disruptive to the community. Warrants a referral and/or monitoring plan. Procedures include:

- Develop and implement a referral plan to get person connected with resources needed to solve problems.
- Address any necessary organizational issues.
- Monitor person and situation if necessary.
- Document investigation, evaluation, and any referral or monitoring.

Priority 4 – Low Risk

Does not appear to pose a threat at this time, and does not exhibit behaviors that are likely to be disruptive to the community. Warrants a monitoring plan to deter escalation. Procedures include:

- Develop and implement a plan to monitor the person/situation for any change.

Priority 5 – No Identified Risk

Does not appear to pose a threat at this time, and no intervention or monitoring is necessary. Close case after proper documentation.

Case Classification and Rationale

Priority Level _____

_____

_____

_____

_____

_____

_____

_____

_____

_____

_____

_____

_____

_____

_____

Next Step:

Proceed to the following section: Case Management and Monitoring.

Case Study 5
Todd Smith

Case Management and Monitoring

Facilitator: If the team decides on a classification level that requires a case management plan—or if they choose a lower level but decide to implement some case management measures—the team should develop and plan how to implement and monitor a case management plan. To prompt them to do so, read aloud the following to the team:

Develop an individualized plan for intervention and monitoring based on the investigation information and other facts known about the person in question. When doing so, take into account the following:

- Case management is more art than science.
- The plan must be fact-based and individualized.
- Engagement is essential, even when dealing with someone who appears very angry. Distancing—including through suspension or expulsion—can make monitoring or intervention particularly difficult.
- Personalities matter. Choose someone the person already trusts, or someone he will like.
- Use the "crew resource management" concept:
    - The team leader may make the ultimate decision, but everyone is obligated to share opinions and raise concerns and ideas.
    - Focus on what still works—for the person and his situation.
    - Focus on what the team, or institution, can change or fix.
    - Think creatively about resources, as well as "eyes and ears."
- Anticipate what might change in the short- and mid-term and how the person may react.
- Management options can include any mix of the following:
    - Outpatient counseling or mental health care
    - Emergency psychiatric evaluation
    - Changes in systemic problems or situations
    - Social skills training
    - Behavioral contract
    - Family involvement
    - Law enforcement involvement
    - Diversion programs
    - Others
- Monitor using available resources. Who sees the person regularly (on and off campus), on weekends, online, etc.?
- Document decision making, implementation, and progress.

Case Management Plan

_____

_____

_____

_____

_____

_____

_____

_____

_____

_____

_____

_____

_____

_____

_____

_____

_____

_____

_____

_____

_____

_____

Case Study 6 – Zeke Dillinger

Initial Report

Facilitator: Print copies of the Key Investigative Questions and Classification Decision sections and distribute them to the team. Then read aloud the following report and questions to the team.

Zeke Dillinger, a student in his second year at the college, wears military fatigues every day. One of his instructors, Melinda Warren, just moved to the area and joined the college faculty this year. Warren reported Dillinger to the team because she thinks he is scary and that it's weird he wears fatigues all the time. Warren said Dillinger's grades are good and that he has one or two friends in her class, but other students find him strange and go out of their way to avoid him. She doesn't want him in her class and wants the team to do something about it.

Initial Team Questions:

1. Based on the information provided, what is the first step the team should take?

2. Is there an imminent situation or a need for the team to call for immediate law enforcement intervention?

3. Is there a need for the team to gather information?

4. If so, where should the team look for information? (Report source requests to the case study facilitator.)

Next Step:

Proceed to the following section: Source Information.

Source Information

Facilitator: Read each source below only when requested by the team; if the team does not think to check certain sources or interview certain people, do not read that information aloud.

Other Instructors

Dillinger is enrolled in three courses at the college. His two other instructors confirmed that Dillinger wears military fatigues every day. His Business II instructor, Zelda Langley, said that she assumed he wears fatigues because he has family in the military, with the college being located in close proximity to a major army base. His auto mechanics instructor, Bobby Gallagher, said that the other students in his class seem to get along fine with Dillinger and that his grades are good. Neither instructor said they have issues with Dillinger's behavior or grades, although Langley said that she was a bit concerned about Dillinger now that the team has asked her because he seems more withdrawn than he did early last year when she taught him in Business I. She thinks it is probably nothing, but she feels better having passed that perception along to the team just in case. She said the only other thing she knows about Dillinger is that last year he had a part-time job at a fast-food restaurant close to campus. She doesn't know if he still has that job or not.

Dillinger's Employer

Dillinger's manager at the fast-food restaurant said that Dillinger has been a good employee for the past two years and has never caused any problems. When asked about the fatigues, the manager said that Dillinger is required to wear a uniform to work, so that has not been an issue. The manager added that Dillinger's father and older brother are both in the army and thought that might be why he wore them. The manager called back later to say that another manager said she is a bit worried about Dillinger because he has seemed a bit quieter and withdrawn in the past few weeks than he usually is. She said "he hasn't been his happy self in a while."

Online Search

An online search on Dillinger's name yielded his Facebook page, which is publicly viewable, with comments from friends over the past two weeks that sound like condolence messages. An earlier status update from Dillinger indicates that his older brother was killed in Afghanistan recently. There have been no status updates since then, with only comments from his Facebook friends. The most recent comments from a few friends ask Dillinger to post an update because they are worried about him.

Dillinger's Friend

The team contacted one of Dillinger's friends, Billy Mackin, who is listed on his Facebook page and also attends the college. Mackin said that Dillinger is taking his brother's death pretty hard and hasn't been the same since. He said that Dillinger lives at home and that his parents are devastated. Dillinger told Mackin that sometimes he wonders what the point of everything is anymore. He also told Mackin that he is really worried about letting his parents know how hopeless he is feeling because his mother is now relying on him for everything, and he is worried that she might get desperate and hurt herself or worse if she feels she can't rely on him. Mackin said he has tried to keep Dillinger distracted by doing fun things, but it doesn't seem to be working. Mackin is starting to feel like he doesn't want to hang out with Dillinger as much because he can be such a downer.

Next Step:

Proceed to the following sections: Key Investigative Questions and then Classification Decision. Make sure the team possesses copies of the pages within these sections.

Key Investigative Questions

As a team, discuss the following specific questions[18] to organize and evaluate the information gathered on the person/situation of concern:

1. **What are Dillinger's motives and goals?**

   ▪ What motivated him to make the statements or take actions that caused him to come to the attention of the team?

   ▪ Does the situation or circumstance that led to these statements or actions still exist?

   ▪ Does he have a major grievance or grudge? Against whom?

   ▪ What efforts have been made to resolve the problem and what has been the result? Does he feel that any part of the problem is resolved or see any alternatives?

2. **Have there been any communications suggesting ideas or an intent to attack?**

   ▪ What, if anything, has Dillinger communicated to someone else (e.g., targets, friends, co-workers, faculty, and family) or written in a diary, journal, e-mail, or website concerning his grievances, ideas, and/or intentions?

   ▪ Have friends been alerted or warned away?

3. **Has Dillinger shown inappropriate interest in any of the following?**

   ▪ Workplace, school, or campus attacks or attackers

   ▪ Weapons (including recent acquisition of any relevant weapon)

   ▪ Incidents of mass violence (e.g., terrorism, workplace violence, and mass murderers)

4. **Has Dillinger engaged in attack-related behaviors?** This means any behavior that moves an idea of violence toward actual violence. Such behaviors might include:

   ▪ Developing an attack idea or plan

   ▪ Making efforts to acquire or practice with weapons

   ▪ Surveying possible sites and areas for attack

   ▪ Testing access to potential targets

   ▪ Rehearsing attacks or ambushes

5. **Does Dillinger have the capacity to carry out an act of targeted violence?**

   ▪ How organized is his thinking and behavior?

   ▪ Does he have the means (e.g., access to a weapon) to carry out an attack?

6. **Is Dillinger experiencing hopelessness, desperation, and/or despair?**

   ▪ Is there information to suggest that he is experiencing desperation and/or despair?

   ▪ Has he experienced a recent failure, loss, and/or loss of status?

   ▪ Is he known to be having difficulty coping with a stressful event?

   ▪ Has he engaged in behavior that suggests he has considered ending his life?

---

18.   Source: Fein et al., *Threat Assessment in Schools* (see n. 7).

7. **Does Dillinger have a trusting relationship with at least one responsible or trustworthy person?**
   - Does he have at least one person he can confide in and believe that person will listen without judging or jumping to conclusions?
   - Is he emotionally connected to other people?
   - Has he previously come to someone's attention or raised concern in a way that suggests he needs intervention or supportive services?

8. **Does Dillinger see violence as the acceptable, desirable, or only way to solve problems?**
   - Does the setting around him (e.g., friends, co-workers, students, parents, and teachers) explicitly or implicitly support or endorse violence as a way of resolving problems or disputes?
   - Has he been dared by others to engage in an act of violence?

9. **Are Dillinger's conversation and story consistent with his actions?**
   - If there is an interview with Dillinger, is his story consistent with behaviors observed by others?

10. **Are other people concerned about Dillinger's potential for violence?**
    - Are those who know him concerned that he might take action based on violent ideas or plans?
    - Are those who know him concerned about a specific target?

11. **What circumstances might affect the likelihood of violence?**
    - What factors in Dillinger's life and/or environment might increase or decrease the likelihood that he will engage in violent behavior?
    - What is the response of others who know about Dillinger's ideas or plans? (Do they actively discourage him from acting violently, encourage him to attack, deny the possibility of violence, or passively collude with an attack?)

12. **Where does Dillinger exist along the "pathway toward violence"?**
    - Has he:
      — Developed an idea to engage in violence?
      — Developed a plan?
      — Taken any steps toward implementing a plan?
      — Developed the capacity or means to carry out the plan?
    - How fast is he moving toward engaging in violence?
    - Where can the team intervene to move Dillinger off the pathway toward violence?

Next Step:

Proceed to the following section: Classification Decision.

Classification Decision

Assessment of Person/Situation

Use the gathered information and the answers to the Key Investigative Questions to answer these ultimate questions:

1. **Does Dillinger pose a threat of harm, whether to himself, to others, or to both? That is, does his behavior suggest that he is on a pathway toward violence?**

   — Has he developed an idea to engage in violence?

   — Has he developed a plan?

   — Has he taken any steps toward implementing the plan?

   — Has he developed the capacity or means to carry out the plan?

   — How fast is he moving toward engaging in violence?

   — Where can the team intervene to move Dillinger off the pathway toward violence?

2. **If Dillinger does not pose a threat of harm, does he otherwise show a need for help or intervention, such as mental health care?**

Priority Risk Scale

Decide how urgent or imminent the situation is, and assign the corresponding classification level using the following priority risk scale:[19]

Priority 1 – Extreme Risk

Appears to pose an imminent threat, and needs immediate containment and eventually case management. Procedures include:

- Contact police/campus security immediately to contain/control person.

- Develop and implement individual case management plan.

- Monitor person, situation, and effectiveness of plan.

- Address any necessary organizational issues.

- Make changes to plan as necessary.

- Discontinue case management when person no longer poses a threat.

- Document investigation, evaluation, plan, and plan implementation.

Priority 2 – High Risk

Appears to pose a non-imminent threat, and requires case management intervention. Procedures include:

- Develop and implement individual case management plan.

- Monitor person, situation, and effectiveness of plan.

- Address any necessary organizational issues.

- Make changes to plan as necessary.

- Discontinue case management when person no longer poses a threat.

- Document investigation, evaluation, plan, and plan implementation.

---

19.   Source: Deisinger et al., *Handbook for Campus Threat Assessment* (see n. 9).

Priority 3 – Moderate Risk

Does not appear to pose a threat at this time, but exhibits behaviors that are likely to be disruptive to the community. Warrants a referral and/or monitoring plan. Procedures include:

- Develop and implement a referral plan to get person connected with resources needed to solve problems.
- Address any necessary organizational issues.
- Monitor person and situation if necessary.
- Document investigation, evaluation, and any referral or monitoring.

Priority 4 – Low Risk

Does not appear to pose a threat at this time, and does not exhibit behaviors that are likely to be disruptive to the community. Warrants a monitoring plan to deter escalation. Procedures include:

- Develop and implement a plan to monitor the person/situation for any change.

Priority 5 – No Identified Risk

Does not appear to pose a threat at this time, and no intervention or monitoring is necessary. Close case after proper documentation.

Case Classification and Rationale

Priority Level _____

_____

_____

_____

_____

_____

_____

_____

_____

_____

_____

_____

_____

_____

_____

_____

Next Step:

Proceed to the following section: Case Management and Monitoring.

Case Management and Monitoring

Facilitator: If the team decides on a classification level that requires a case management plan—or if they choose a lower level but decide to implement some case management measures—the team should develop and plan how to implement and monitor a case management plan. To prompt them to do so, read aloud the following to the team:

Develop an individualized plan for intervention and monitoring based on the investigation information and other facts known about the person in question. When doing so, take into account the following:

- Case management is more art than science.
- The plan must be fact-based and individualized.
- Engagement is essential, even when dealing with someone who appears very angry. Distancing—including through suspension or expulsion—can make monitoring or intervention particularly difficult.
- Personalities matter. Choose someone the person already trusts, or someone he will like.
- Use the "crew resource management" concept:
  - The team leader may make the ultimate decision, but everyone is obligated to share opinions and raise concerns and ideas.
  - Focus on what still works—for the person and his situation.
  - Focus on what the team, or institution, can change or fix.
  - Think creatively about resources, as well as "eyes and ears."
- Anticipate what might change in the short- and mid-term and how the person may react.
- Management options can include any mix of the following:
  - Outpatient counseling or mental health care
  - Emergency psychiatric evaluation
  - Mentoring relationship
  - Academic accommodations (if the student has a documented disability; also consider "academic relief" according to the institution's policy)
  - Suspension or expulsion
  - Voluntary medical leave
  - Changes in systemic problems or situations
  - Social skills training
  - Behavioral contract
  - Family involvement
  - Law enforcement involvement
  - Diversion programs
  - Management by walking around or through appropriate alliances
  - Others
- Monitor using available resources. Who sees the person regularly (on and off campus), on weekends, online, etc.?
- Document decision making, implementation, and progress.

Case Management Plan

Case Study 7 – Donald Martin

Initial Report
Facilitator: Print copies of the Key Investigative Questions and Classification Decision sections and distribute them to the team. Then read aloud the following report and questions to the team.

An alumnus of the college, Andy Newman, called the campus police department to report a concern about a former student, Donald Martin. Newman knew Martin while they attended the college together, and they have stayed in touch via Facebook since Newman graduated in 2008. Martin was enrolled at the college until 2008 but did not graduate; he completed all of his coursework but failed his senior-year political science course and was not granted a degree. In recent weeks, Martin's Facebook status updates have led Newman to become concerned about Martin and a fixation he seems to have on the college. Newman said that posts starting three weeks ago led him to think that Martin may have been fired from his job and is now blaming the college. Newman said that he was casual friends with Martin in college, that they were not that close, and that they have exchanged only a few messages on Facebook since then. He thinks Martin might still live at home with his mother, but he isn't sure. Newman asked that the campus police department not let Martin know who reported him.

Initial Team Questions:
1. Based on the information provided, what is the first step the team should take?
2. Is there an imminent situation or a need for the team to call for immediate law enforcement intervention?
3. Is there a need for the team to gather information?
4. If so, where should the team look for information? (Report source requests to the case study facilitator.)

Next Step:
Proceed to the following section: Source Information.

Source Information

Facilitator: Read each source below only when requested by the team; if the team does not think to check certain sources or interview certain people, do not read that information aloud.

Facebook Posts

Through Newman, the threat assessment team reviewed Martin's Facebook page and his postings over the past several months. Just as Newman described, Martin's posts reference him losing his job a few weeks ago, and several recent posts suggest Martin blames the college and, in particular, his former political science professor, Doug Woodruff, for why he lost his job. Martin's most recent post, from the day before yesterday, said, "Donald Martin is thinking about getting even…once and for all." Photos posted by Martin include several of him shooting various weapons at an indoor firing range.

Martin's Former Employer

The human resources director of Martin's former employer, a prominent silicon valley-based computer software company, returned the team's call with a message that confirms the dates of Martin's employment but provides no further information. Two subsequent messages left for the director have not been returned.

Online Search – Martin's Name

An online search on Martin's name yielded a Twitter account that is publicly viewable, along with the Facebook page that Newman reported to the police department. The Twitter posts from the past three weeks are identical to the Facebook page posts, suggesting that Martin's posts to Twitter automatically update his Facebook page.

Online Search – College's Name

An online search on the name of the college yielded several chat forums with negative commentary about the college from several posters, but they discuss a range of budgetary cutback decisions made by the college in the previous 12 months. It is not clear which—if any—of those postings on the forums are Martin's.

Online Search – Professor's Name (Doug Woodruff)

An online search on Woodruff's name revealed a website with the domain name DougWoodruff.net. The page includes many negative comments about Woodruff and calls him a "career killer." A follow-up WhoIs search on the domain name indicated that the domain name was purchased within the past month and the owner is a D. Martin.

Martin's Mother

Martin's mother was willing to speak about her son because the threat assessment team members said they were inquiring about his welfare. She said she is sure the team members are wrong about Martin losing his job because he goes to work every day and she would have heard if he lost his job. She said he has seemed somewhat angry lately but that is because his girlfriend recently broke up with him. But Martin's mother isn't worried about him because he had a lot of girlfriends in college and she is sure he will be dating again very soon.

Martin's Ex-Girlfriend

Martin's ex-girlfriend said she is worried about him because he had become increasingly angry over the past few weeks, ever since he was fired from his job, and all he could talk about was how he would still have his job and his career if not for the professor who failed him in his senior year of college. She said Martin's employer had started requiring all of their programmers to have college degrees; they offered to give him a flexible work schedule to go back and complete his degree, but he became irate and threatened his supervisor, so they fired him.

Next Step:

Proceed to the following sections: Key Investigative Questions and then Classification Decision. Make sure the team possesses copies of the pages within these sections.

Key Investigative Questions

As a team, discuss the following specific questions[20] to organize and evaluate the information gathered on the person/situation of concern:

1. **What are Martin's motives and goals?**

   - What motivated him to make the statements or take actions that caused him to come to the attention of the team?

   - Does the situation or circumstance that led to these statements or actions still exist?

   - Does he have a major grievance or grudge? Against whom?

   - What efforts have been made to resolve the problem and what has been the result? Does he feel that any part of the problem is resolved or see any alternatives?

2. **Have there been any communications suggesting ideas or an intent to attack?**

   - What, if anything, has Martin communicated to someone else (e.g., targets, friends, co-workers, faculty, and family) or written in a diary, journal, e-mail, or website concerning his grievances, ideas, and/or intentions?

   - Have friends been alerted or warned away?

3. **Has Martin shown inappropriate interest in any of the following?**

   - Workplace, school, or campus attacks or attackers

   - Weapons (including recent acquisition of any relevant weapon)

   - Incidents of mass violence (e.g., terrorism, workplace violence, and mass murderers)

4. **Has Martin engaged in attack-related behaviors?** This means any behavior that moves an idea of violence toward actual violence. Such behaviors might include:

   - Developing an attack idea or plan

   - Making efforts to acquire or practice with weapons

   - Surveying possible sites and areas for attack

   - Testing access to potential targets

   - Rehearsing attacks or ambushes

5. **Does Martin have the capacity to carry out an act of targeted violence?**

   - How organized is his thinking and behavior?

   - Does he have the means (e.g., access to a weapon) to carry out an attack?

6. **Is Martin experiencing hopelessness, desperation, and/or despair?**

   - Is there information to suggest that he is experiencing desperation and/or despair?

   - Has he experienced a recent failure, loss, and/or loss of status?

   - Is Donald known to be having difficulty coping with a stressful event?

   - Has he engaged in behavior that suggests he has considered ending his life?

---

20.   Source: Fein et al., *Threat Assessment in Schools* (see n. 7).

7. **Does Martin have a trusting relationship with at least one responsible or trustworthy person?**

   * Does he have at least one person he can confide in and believe that person will listen without judging or jumping to conclusions?

   * Is he emotionally connected to other people?

   * Has he previously come to someone's attention or raised concern in a way that suggests he needs intervention or supportive services?

8. **Does Martin see violence as the acceptable, desirable, or only way to solve problems?**

   * Does the setting around him (e.g., friends, co-workers, students, parents, and teachers) explicitly or implicitly support or endorse violence as a way of resolving problems or disputes?

   * Has he been dared by others to engage in an act of violence?

9. **Are Martin's conversation and story consistent with his actions?**

   * If there is an interview with Martin, is his story consistent with behaviors observed by others?

10. **Are other people concerned about Martin's potential for violence?**

    * Are those who know him concerned that he might take action based on violent ideas or plans?

    * Are those who know him concerned about a specific target?

11. **What circumstances might affect the likelihood of violence?**

    * What factors in Martin's life and/or environment might increase or decrease the likelihood that he will engage in violent behavior?

    * What is the response of others who know about Martin's ideas or plans? (Do they actively discourage him from acting violently, encourage him to attack, deny the possibility of violence, or passively collude with an attack?)

12. **Where does Martin exist along the "pathway toward violence"?**

    * Has he:

        — Developed an idea to engage in violence?

        — Developed a plan?

        — Taken any steps toward implementing a plan?

        — Developed the capacity or means to carry out the plan?

    * How fast is he moving toward engaging in violence?

    * Where can the team intervene to move Martin off the pathway toward violence?

Next Step:

Proceed to the following section: Classification Decision.

Classification Decision

Assessment of Person/Situation

Use the gathered information and the answers to the Key Investigative Questions to answer these ultimate questions:

1. **Does Martin pose a threat of harm, whether to himself, to others, or to both? That is, does his behavior suggest that he is on a pathway toward violence?**

   - Has he developed an idea to engage in violence?
   - Has he developed a plan?
   - Has he taken any steps toward implementing the plan?
   - Has he developed the capacity or means to carry out the plan?
   - How fast is he moving toward engaging in violence?
   - Where can the team intervene to move Martin off the pathway toward violence?

2. **If Martin does not pose a threat of harm, does he otherwise show a need for help or intervention, such as mental health care?**

Priority Risk Scale

Decide how urgent or imminent the situation is, and assign the corresponding classification level using the following priority risk scale:[21]

Priority 1 – Extreme Risk

Appears to pose an imminent threat, and needs immediate containment and eventually case management. Procedures include:

- Contact police/campus security immediately to contain/control person.
- Develop and implement individual case management plan.
- Monitor person, situation, and effectiveness of plan.
- Address any necessary organizational issues.
- Make changes to plan as necessary.
- Discontinue case management when person no longer poses a threat.
- Document investigation, evaluation, plan, and plan implementation.

Priority 2 – High Risk

Appears to pose a non-imminent threat, and requires case management intervention. Procedures include:

- Develop and implement individual case management plan.
- Monitor person, situation, and effectiveness of plan.
- Address any necessary organizational issues.
- Make changes to plan as necessary.
- Discontinue case management when person no longer poses a threat.
- Document investigation, evaluation, plan, and plan implementation.

---

21.   Source: Deisinger et al., *Handbook for Campus Threat Assessment* (see n. 9).

Priority 3 – Moderate Risk

Does not appear to pose a threat at this time, but exhibits behaviors that are likely to be disruptive to the community. Warrants a referral and/or monitoring plan. Procedures include:

- Develop and implement a referral plan to get person connected with resources needed to solve problems.
- Address any necessary organizational issues.
- Monitor person and situation if necessary.
- Document investigation, evaluation, and any referral or monitoring.

Priority 4 – Low Risk

Does not appear to pose a threat at this time, and does not exhibit behaviors that are likely to be disruptive to the community. Warrants a monitoring plan to deter escalation. Procedures include:

- Develop and implement a plan to monitor the person/situation for any change.

Priority 5 – No Identified Risk

Does not appear to pose a threat at this time, and no intervention or monitoring is necessary. Close case after proper documentation.

Case Classification and Rationale

Priority Level _____

_____

_____

_____

_____

_____

_____

_____

_____

_____

_____

_____

_____

Next Step:

Proceed to the following section: Case Management and Monitoring.

Case Management and Monitoring

Facilitator: If the team decides on a classification level that requires a case management plan—or if they choose a lower level but decide to implement some case management measures—the team should develop and plan how to implement and monitor a case management plan. To prompt them to do so, read aloud the following to the team:

Develop an individualized plan for intervention and monitoring based on the investigation information and other facts known about the person in question. When doing so, take into account the following:

- Case management is more art than science.
- The plan must be fact-based and individualized.
- Engagement is essential, even when dealing with someone who appears very angry. Distancing—including through suspension or expulsion—can make monitoring or intervention particularly difficult.
- Personalities matter. Choose someone the person already trusts, or someone he will like.
- Use the "crew resource management" concept:
    — The team leader may make the ultimate decision, but everyone is obligated to share opinions and raise concerns and ideas.
    — Focus on what still works—for the person and his situation.
    — Focus on what the team, or institution, can change or fix.
    — Think creatively about resources, as well as "eyes and ears."
- Anticipate what might change in the short- and mid-term and how the person may react.
- Management options can include any mix of the following:
    — Outpatient counseling or mental health care
    — Emergency psychiatric evaluation
    — Mentoring relationship
    — Changes in systemic problems or situations
    — Social skills training
    — Behavioral contract
    — Family involvement
    — Law enforcement involvement
    — Diversion programs
    — Others
- Monitor using available resources. Who sees the person regularly (on and off campus), on weekends, online, etc.?
- Document decision making, implementation, and progress.

Case Management Plan

Case Study 8 – Anonymous

Initial Report

Facilitator: Print copies of the Key Investigative Questions and Classification Decision sections and distribute them to the team. Then read aloud the following report and questions to the team.

Several reports came in to the campus police department and the threat assessment team from students who saw videos posted on YouTube by some-one using the screen name Doomsday2012. The content of the videos shows a masked man standing with a weapon in front of a mirror, taping himself, and using some method to distort his voice. The videos are short and focus on the man's dream of carrying out a Virginia Tech-style attack on the college. After the campus police department contacted YouTube, YouTube administrators took down the videos, blocked Doomsday2012's account, and preserved the page as evidence. YouTube also traced the IP address from which the videos were posted and reported that the address comes from somewhere in China.

Initial Team Questions:

1. Based on the information provided, what is the first step the team should take?

2. Is there an imminent situation or a need for the team to call for immediate law enforcement intervention?

3. Is there a need for the team to gather information?

4. If so, where should the team look for information? (Report source requests to the case study facilitator.)

Next Step:

Proceed to the following section: Source Information.

Source Information

Facilitator: Read each source below only when requested by the team; if the team does not think to check certain sources or interview certain people, do not read that information aloud.

Online Search – Doomsday2012

An online search on Doomsday2012 yielded only cached pages from his video posts on YouTube. There is no other information available.

Online Search – College's Name

An online search on the name of the college shows no unusual or concerning content.

Suggestions from the Team

With so little investigative information available, what are the team's next steps?

1. _____

_____

_____

2. _____

_____

_____

3. _____

_____

_____

4. _____

_____

_____

5. _____

_____

_____

Next Step:

Proceed to the following sections: Key Investigative Questions and then Classification Decision. Make sure the team possesses copies of the pages within these sections.

Key Investigative Questions

As a team, discuss the following specific questions[22] to organize and evaluate the information gathered on the person/situation of concern:

1. **What are the person's motives and goals?**
   - What motivated him to make the statements or take actions that caused him to come to the attention of the team?
   - Does the situation or circumstance that led to these statements or actions still exist?
   - Does he have a major grievance or grudge? Against whom?
   - What efforts have been made to resolve the problem and what has been the result? Does the person feel that any part of the problem is resolved or see any alternatives?

2. **Have there been any communications suggesting ideas or an intent to attack?**
   - What, if anything, has the person communicated to someone else (e.g., targets, friends, co-workers, faculty, and family) or written in a diary, journal, e-mail, or website concerning his grievances, ideas, and/or intentions?
   - Have friends been alerted or warned away?

3. **Has the person shown inappropriate interest in any of the following?**
   - Workplace, school, or campus attacks or attackers
   - Weapons (including recent acquisition of any relevant weapon)
   - Incidents of mass violence (e.g., terrorism, workplace violence, and mass murderers)

4. **Has the person engaged in attack-related behaviors?** This means any behavior that moves an idea of violence toward actual violence. Such behaviors might include:
   - Developing an attack idea or plan
   - Making efforts to acquire or practice with weapons
   - Surveying possible sites and areas for attack
   - Testing access to potential targets
   - Rehearsing attacks or ambushes

5. **Does the person have the capacity to carry out an act of targeted violence?**
   - How organized is his thinking and behavior?
   - Does he have the means (e.g., access to a weapon) to carry out an attack?

6. **Is the person experiencing hopelessness, desperation, and/or despair?**
   - Is there information to suggest that he is experiencing desperation and/or despair?
   - Has he experienced a recent failure, loss, and/or loss of status?
   - Is the person known to be having difficulty coping with a stressful event?
   - Has he engaged in behavior that suggests he has considered ending his life?

---

22.   Source: Fein et al., *Threat Assessment in Schools* (see n. 7).

7. **Does the person have a trusting relationship with at least one responsible or trustworthy person?**
   - Does he have at least one person he can confide in and believe that person will listen without judging or jumping to conclusions?
   - Is he emotionally connected to other people?
   - Has he previously come to someone's attention or raised concern in a way that suggests he needs intervention or supportive services?

8. **Does the person see violence as the acceptable, desirable, or only way to solve problems?**
   - Does the setting around him (e.g., friends, co-workers, students, parents, and teachers) explicitly or implicitly support or endorse violence as a way of resolving problems or disputes?
   - Has he been dared by others to engage in an act of violence?

9. **Are the person's conversation and story consistent with his actions?**
   - If there is an interview with the person, is his story consistent with behaviors observed by others?

10. **Are other people concerned about the person's potential for violence?**
    - Are those who know him concerned that he might take action based on violent ideas or plans?
    - Are those who know him concerned about a specific target?

11. **What circumstances might affect the likelihood of violence?**
    - What factors in the person's life and/or environment might increase or decrease the likelihood that he will engage in violent behavior?
    - What is the response of others who know about the person's ideas or plans? (Do they actively discourage him from acting violently, encourage him to attack, deny the possibility of violence, or passively collude with an attack?)

12. **Where does the person exist along the "pathway toward violence"?**
    - Has he:
        - Developed an idea to engage in violence?
        - Developed a plan?
        - Taken any steps toward implementing a plan?
        - Developed the capacity or means to carry out the plan?
    - How fast is he moving toward engaging in violence?
    - Where can the team intervene to move the person off the pathway toward violence?

Next Step:

Proceed to the following section: Classification Decision.

Classification Decision

Assessment of Person/Situation

Use the gathered information and the answers to the Key Investigative Questions to answer these ultimate questions:

1. **Does the person pose a threat of harm, whether to himself, to others, or to both? That is, does his behavior suggest that he is on a pathway toward violence?**

    — Has he developed an idea to engage in violence?

    — Has he developed a plan?

    — Has he taken any steps toward implementing the plan?

    — Has he developed the capacity or means to carry out the plan?

    — How fast is he moving toward engaging in violence?

    — Where can the team intervene to move the person off the pathway toward violence?

2. **If the person does not pose a threat of harm, does he otherwise show a need for help or intervention, such as mental health care?**

Priority Risk Scale

Decide how urgent or imminent the situation is, and assign the corresponding classification level using the following priority risk scale:[23]

Priority 1 – Extreme Risk

Appears to pose an imminent threat, and needs immediate containment and eventually case management. Procedures include:

- Contact police/campus security immediately to contain/control person.
- Develop and implement individual case management plan.
- Monitor person, situation, and effectiveness of plan.
- Address any necessary organizational issues.
- Make changes to plan as necessary.
- Discontinue case management when person no longer poses a threat.
- Document investigation, evaluation, plan, and plan implementation.

Priority 2 – High Risk

Appears to pose a non-imminent threat, and requires case management intervention. Procedures include:

- Develop and implement individual case management plan.
- Monitor person, situation, and effectiveness of plan.
- Address any necessary organizational issues.
- Make changes to plan as necessary.
- Discontinue case management when person no longer poses a threat.
- Document investigation, evaluation, plan, and plan implementation.

---

23.   Source: Deisinger et al., *Handbook for Campus Threat Assessment* (see n. 9).

Priority 3 – Moderate Risk

Does not appear to pose a threat at this time, but exhibits behaviors that are likely to be disruptive to the community. Warrants a referral and/or monitoring plan. Procedures include:

- Develop and implement a referral plan to get person connected with resources needed to solve problems.
- Address any necessary organizational issues.
- Monitor person and situation if necessary.
- Document investigation, evaluation, and any referral or monitoring.

Priority 4 – Low Risk

Does not appear to pose a threat at this time, and does not exhibit behaviors that are likely to be disruptive to the community. Warrants a monitoring plan to deter escalation. Procedures include:

- Develop and implement a plan to monitor the person/situation for any change.

Priority 5 – No Identified Risk

Does not appear to pose a threat at this time, and no intervention or monitoring is necessary. Close case after proper documentation.

Case Classification and Rationale

Priority Level _____

_____

_____

_____

_____

_____

_____

_____

_____

_____

_____

_____

_____

_____

_____

Next Step:

Proceed to the following section: Case Management and Monitoring.

Case Management and Monitoring

Facilitator: If the team decides on a classification level that requires a case management plan—or if they choose a lower level but decide to implement some case management measures—the team should develop and plan how to implement and monitor a case management plan. To prompt them to do so, read aloud the following to the team:

Develop an individualized plan for intervention and monitoring based on the investigation information and other facts known about the person in question. When doing so, take into account the following:

- Case management is more art than science.
- The plan must be fact-based and individualized.
- Engagement is essential, even when dealing with someone who appears very angry. Distancing—including through suspension or expulsion—can make monitoring or intervention particularly difficult.
- Personalities matter. Choose someone the person already trusts, or someone he will like.
- Use the "crew resource management" concept:
  - The team leader may make the ultimate decision, but everyone is obligated to share opinions and raise concerns and ideas.
  - Focus on what still works—for the person and his situation.
  - Focus on what the team, or institution, can change or fix.
  - Think creatively about resources, as well as "eyes and ears."
- Anticipate what might change in the short- and mid-term and how the person may react.
- Management options can include any mix of the following:
  - Outpatient counseling and mental health care
  - Emergency psychiatric evaluation
  - Mentoring relationship
  - Academic accommodations (if the student has a documented disability; also consider "academic relief" according to the institution's policy)
  - Suspension or expulsion
  - Voluntary medical leave
  - Changes in systemic problems or situations
  - Social skills training
  - Behavioral contract
  - Family involvement
  - Law enforcement involvement
  - Diversion programs
  - Management by walking around or through appropriate alliances
  - Others
- Monitor using available resources. Who sees the person regularly (on and off campus), on weekends, online, etc.?
- Document decision making, implementation, and progress.

Case Management Plan

About the COPS Office

The Office of Community Oriented Policing Services (COPS Office) is the component of the U.S. Department of Justice responsible for advancing the practice of community policing by the nation's state, local, territory, and tribal law enforcement agencies through information and grant resources.

Community policing is a philosophy that promotes organizational strategies that support the systematic use of partnerships and problem-solving techniques, to proactively address the immediate conditions that give rise to public safety issues such as crime, social disorder, and fear of crime.

Rather than simply responding to crimes once they have been committed, community policing concentrates on preventing crime and eliminating the atmosphere of fear it creates. Earning the trust of the community and making those individuals stakeholders in their own safety enables law enforcement to better understand and address both the needs of the community and the factors that contribute to crime.

The COPS Office awards grants to state, local, territory, and tribal law enforcement agencies to hire and train community policing professionals, acquire and deploy cutting-edge crime fighting technologies, and develop and test innovative policing strategies. COPS Office funding also provides training and technical assistance to community members and local government leaders and all levels of law enforcement. The COPS Office has produced and compiled a broad range of information resources that can help law enforcement better address specific crime and operational issues, and help community leaders better understand how to work cooperatively with their law enforcement agency to reduce crime.

- Since 1994, the COPS Office has invested nearly $14 billion to add community policing officers to the nation's streets, enhance crime fighting technology, support crime prevention initiatives, and provide training and technical assistance to help advance community policing.
- By the end of FY2011, the COPS Office has funded approximately 123,000 additional officers to more than 13,000 of the nation's 18,000 law enforcement agencies across the country in small and large jurisdictions alike.
- Nearly 600,000 law enforcement personnel, community members, and government leaders have been trained through COPS Office-funded training organizations.
- As of 2011, the COPS Office has distributed more than 6.6 million topic-specific publications, training curricula, white papers, and resource CDs.

COPS Office resources, covering a wide breadth of community policing topics—from school and campus safety to gang violence—are available, at no cost, through its online Resource Information Center at www.cops.usdoj.gov. This easy-to-navigate website is also the grant application portal, providing access to online application forms.

Made in the USA
Lexington, KY
15 June 2018